The Essential Anatomy of Melancholy

Robert Burton

ACCOUNT OF THE AUTHOR.

Robert Burton was the son of Ralph Burton, of an ancient and genteel family at Lindley, in Leicestershire, and was born there on the 8th of February 1576. [1]He received the first rudiments of learning at the free school of Sutton Coldfield, in Warwickshire [2]from whence he was, at the age of seventeen, in the long vacation, 1593, sent to Brazen Nose College, in the condition of a commoner, where he made considerable progress in logic and philosophy. In 1599 he was elected student of Christ Church, and, for form's sake, was put under the tuition of Dr. John Bancroft, afterwards Bishop of Oxford. In 1614 he was admitted to the reading of the Sentences, and on the 29th of November, 1616, had the vicarage of St. Thomas, in the west suburb of Oxford, conferred on him by the dean and canons of Christ Church, which, with the rectory of Segrave, in Leicestershire, given to him in the year 1636, by George, Lord Berkeley, he kept, to use the words of the Oxford antiquary, with much ado to his dying day. He seems to have been first beneficed at Walsby, in Lincolnshire, through the munificence of his noble patroness, Frances, Countess Dowager of Exeter, but resigned the same, as he tells us, for some special reasons. At his vicarage he is remarked to have always given the sacrament in wafers. Wood's character of him is, that he was an exact mathematician, a curious calculator of nativities, a general read scholar, a thorough-paced philologist, and one that understood the surveying of lands well. As he was by many accounted a severe student, a devourer of authors, a melancholy and humorous person; so by others, who knew him well, a person of great honesty, plain dealing and charity. I have heard some of the ancients of Christ Church often say, that his company was very merry, facete, and juvenile; and no man in his time did surpass him for his ready and dexterous interlarding his common discourses among them with verses from the poets, or sentences from classic authors; which being then all the fashion in the University, made his company the more acceptable. He appears to have been a universal reader of all kinds of books, and availed himself of his multifarious studies in a very extraordinary manner. From the information of Hearne, we learn that John Rouse, the Bodleian librarian, furnished him with choice books for the prosecution of his work. The subject of his labour and amusement, seems to have been adopted from the infirmities of his own habit and constitution. Mr. Granger says, He composed this book with a view of relieving his own melancholy, but increased it to such a degree, that nothing could make him laugh, but going to the bridge-foot and hearing the ribaldry of the bargemen, which rarely failed to throw him into a violent fit of laughter. Before he was overcome with this horrid disorder, he, in the intervals of his vapours, was esteemed one of the most facetious companions in the University.

His residence was chiefly at Oxford; where, in his chamber in Christ Church College, he departed this life, at or very near the time which he had some years before foretold, from the calculation of his own nativity, and which, says Wood, being exact, several of the students did not

forbear to whisper among themselves, that rather than there should be a mistake in the calculation, he sent up his soul to heaven through a slip about his neck. Whether this suggestion is founded in truth, we have no other evidence than an obscure hint in the epitaph hereafter inserted, which was written by the author himself, a short time before his death. His body, with due solemnity, was buried near that of Dr. Robert Weston, in the north aisle which joins next to the choir of the cathedral of Christ Church, on the 27th of January 1639-40. Over his grave was soon after erected a comely monument, on the upper pillar of the said aisle, with his bust, painted to the life. On the right hand is the following calculation of his nativity:
and under the bust, this inscription of his own composition:— Paucis notus, paucioribus ignotus,
Hic jacet *Democritus* junior
Cui vitam dedit et mortem
Melancholia
Ob. 8 Id. Jan. A. C. MDCXXXIX.
Arms:—Azure on a bend O. between three dogs' heads O. a crescent G.
A few months before his death, he made his will, of which the following is a copy:

EXTRACTED FROM THE REGISTRY OF THE PREROGATIVE COURT OF CANTERBURY.

In nomine Dei Amen. August 15th One thousand six hundred thirty nine because there be so many casualties to which our life is subject besides quarrelling and contention which happen to our Successors after our Death by reason of unsettled Estates I Robert Burton Student of Christchurch Oxon. though my means be but small have thought good by this my last Will and Testament to dispose of that little which I have and being at this present I thank God in perfect health of Bodie and Mind and if this Testament be not so formal according to the nice and strict terms of Law and other Circumstances peradventure required of which I am ignorant I desire howsoever this my Will may be accepted and stand good according to my true Intent and meaning First I bequeath Animam Deo Corpus Terrae whensoever it shall please God to call me I give my Land in Higham which my good Father Ralphe Burton of Lindly in the County of Leicester Esquire gave me by Deed of Gift and that which I have annexed to that Farm by purchase since, now leased for thirty eight pounds per Ann. to mine Elder Brother William Burton of Lindly Esquire during his life and after him to his Heirs I make my said Brother William likewise mine Executor as well as paying such Annuities and Legacies out of my Lands and Goods as are hereafter specified I give to my nephew Cassibilan Burton twenty pounds Annuity per Ann. out of my Land in Higham during his life to be paid at two equal payments at our Lady Day in Lent and Michaelmas or if he be not paid within fourteen Days after the said Feasts to distrain on any part of the Ground or on any of my Lands of Inheritance Item I give to my Sister Katherine Jackson during her life eight pounds per Ann. Annuity to be paid at the two Feasts equally as above said or else to distrain on the Ground if she be not paid after fourteen days at Lindly as the other *some* is out of the said Land Item I give to my Servant John Upton the Annuity of Forty Shillings out of my said Farme during his life (if till then my Servant) to be paid on Michaelmas day in Lindley each year or else after fourteen days to distrain Now for my goods I thus dispose them First I give an C'th pounds to Christ Church in Oxford where I have so long lived to buy five pounds Lands per Ann. to be Yearly bestowed on Books for the Library Item I give an hundredth pound to the University Library of Oxford to be bestowed to purchase five pound Land per Ann. to be paid out Yearly on Books as Mrs. Brooks formerly gave an hundred pounds to buy Land to the same purpose and the Rent to the same use I give to my Brother George Burton twenty pounds and my watch I give to my Brother Ralph Burton five pounds Item I give to the Parish of Seagrave in Leicestershire where I am now Rector ten pounds to be given to a certain Feoffees to the perpetual good of the said *Parish Oxon [3]*Item I give to my Niece Eugenia Burton One hundredth pounds Item I give to my Nephew Richard Burton now Prisoner in London an hundredth pound to redeem him Item I give to the Poor of Higham Forty Shillings where my Land is to the poor of Nuneaton where I was once a Grammar Scholar three pound to my Cousin Purfey of Wadlake [Wadley] my Cousin Purfey of Calcott my Cousin Hales of Coventry my Nephew Bradshaw of Orton twenty shillings a piece for a small remembrance to Mr. Whitehall Rector of Cherkby myne own Chamber Fellow twenty shillings I desire my Brother George and my Cosen Purfey of Calcott to be the Overseers of this part of my Will I give moreover five pounds to make a small Monument for my Mother where she is buried in London to my Brother Jackson forty shillings to my Servant John Upton forty shillings besides his former Annuity if he be my Servant till I die if he be till then my Servant *[4]—* ROBERT BURTON—Charles Russell Witness—John Pepper Witness. An Appendix to this my Will if I die in Oxford or whilst I am of Christ Church and with good Mr. Paynes August the Fifteenth 1639. I give to Mr. Doctor Fell Dean of Christ Church Forty Shillings to the Eight Canons twenty Shillings a piece as a small remembrance to the poor of St. Thomas Parish Twenty Shillings to Brasenose Library five pounds to Mr. Rowse of Oriell Colledge twenty Shillings to Mr. Heywood *xx*s. to Dr. Metcalfe *xx*s. to Mr. Sherley *xx*s. If I have any Books the University Library hath not, let them take them If I have any Books our own Library hath not, let them take them I give to Mrs. Fell all my English Books of Husbandry one excepted to her Daughter Mrs. Katherine Fell my Six Pieces of Silver Plate and six Silver spoons to Mrs. Iles my Gerards Herball To Mrs. Morris my Country Farme Translated out of French 4. and all my English Physick Books to Mr. Whistler the Recorder of Oxford I give twenty shillings to all my fellow Students Mrs of Arts a Book in fol. or two a piece as Master Morris Treasurer or Mr. Dean shall appoint whom I request to be the Overseer of this Appendix and give him for his pains Atlas Geografer and Ortelius Theatrum Mond' I give to John Fell the Dean's Son Student my Mathematical Instruments except my two Crosse Staves which I give to my Lord of Donnol if he be then of the House To Thomas Iles Doctor Iles his Son Student Saluntch on Paurrhelia and Lucian's Works in 4 Tomes If any books be left let my Executors dispose of them with all such Books as are written with my own hands and half my Melancholy Copy for Crips hath the other half To Mr. Jones Chaplin and Chanter my Surveying Books and Instruments To the Servants of the House Forty Shillings ROB. BURTON—Charles Russell Witness—John Pepper Witness—This Will was shewed to me by the Testator and acknowledged by him some few days before his death to be his last Will Ita Testor John Morris S Th D. Prebendari' Eccl Chri' Oxon Feb. 3, 1639.

Probatum fuit Testamentum suprascriptum, &c. 11° 1640 Juramento Willmi Burton Fris' et Executoris cui &c. de bene et fideliter administrand. &c. coram Mag'ris Nathanaele Stephens Rectore Eccl. de Drayton, et Edwardo Farmer, Clericis, vigore commissionis, &c.

The only work our author executed was that now reprinted, which probably was the principal employment of his life. Dr. Ferriar says, it was originally published in the year 1617; but this is evidently a mistake; [5]the first edition was that printed in 4to, 1621, a copy of which is at present in the collection of John Nichols, Esq., the indefatigable illustrator of the *History of Leicestershire*; to whom, and to Isaac Reed, Esq., of Staple Inn, this account is greatly indebted for its accuracy. The other impressions of it were in 1624, 1628, 1632, 1638, 1651-2, 1660, and 1676, which last, in the titlepage, is called the eighth edition.

The copy from which the present is reprinted, is that of 1651-2; at the conclusion of which is the following address:

"TO THE READER.

Be pleased to know (Courteous Reader) that since the last Impression of this Book, the ingenuous Author of it is deceased, leaving a Copy of it exactly corrected, with several considerable Additions by his own hand; this Copy he committed to my care and custody, with directions to have those Additions inserted in the next Edition; which in order to his command, and the Publicke Good, is faithfully performed in this last Impression.

H. C. (*i.e. HEN. CRIPPS.*)

The following testimonies of various authors will serve to show the estimation in which this work has been held:—

The ANATOMY OF MELANCHOLY, wherein the author hath piled up variety of much excellent learning. Scarce any book of philology in our land hath, in so short a time, passed so many editions.—*Fuller's Worthies*, fol. 16.

'Tis a book so full of variety of reading, that gentlemen who have lost their time, and are put to a push for invention, may furnish themselves with matter for common or scholastical discourse and writing.—*Wood's Athenae Oxoniensis*, vol. i. p. 628. 2d edit.

If you never saw BURTON UPON MELANCHOLY, printed 1676, I pray look into it, and read the ninth page of his Preface, 'Democritus to the Reader.' There is something there which touches the point we are upon; but I mention the author to you, as the pleasantest, the most learned, and the most full of sterling sense. The wits of Queen Anne's reign, and the beginning of George the First, were not a little beholden to him.— *Archbishop Herring's Letters*, 12mo. 1777. p. 149.

BURTON'S ANATOMY OF MELANCHOLY, he (Dr. Johnson) said, was the only book that ever took him out of bed two hours sooner than he wished to rise.—*Boswell's Life of Johnson*, vol. i. p. 580. 8vo. edit.

BURTON'S ANATOMY OF MELANCHOLY is a valuable book, said Dr. Johnson. It is, perhaps, overloaded with quotation. But there is great spirit and great power in what Burton says when he writes from his own mind.—*Ibid*, vol. ii. p. 325.

It will be no detraction from the powers of Milton's original genius and invention, to remark, that he seems to have borrowed the subject of *L' Allegro* and *Il Penseroso*, together with some particular thoughts, expressions, and rhymes, more especially the idea of a contrast between these two dispositions, from a forgotten poem prefixed to the first edition of BURTON'S ANATOMY OF MELANCHOLY, entitled, 'The Author's Abstract of Melancholy; or, A Dialogue between Pleasure and Pain.' Here pain is melancholy. It was written, as I conjecture, about the year 1600. I will make no apology for abstracting and citing as much of this poem as will be sufficient to prove, to a discerning reader, how far it had taken possession of Milton's mind. The measure will appear to be the same; and that our author was at least an attentive reader of Burton's book, may be already concluded from the traces of resemblance which I have incidentally noticed in passing through the *L' Allegro* and *Il Penseroso*.— After extracting the lines, Mr. Warton adds, as to the very elaborate work to which these visionary verses are no unsuitable introduction, the writer's variety of learning, his quotations from scarce and curious books, his pedantry sparkling with rude wit and shapeless elegance, miscellaneous matter, intermixture of agreeable tales and illustrations, and, perhaps, above all, the singularities of his feelings, clothed in an uncommon quaintness of style, have contributed to render it, even to modern readers, a valuable repository of amusement and information.— *Warton's Milton*, 2d edit. p. 94.

THE ANATOMY OF MELANCHOLY is a book which has been universally read and admired. This work is, for the most part, what the author himself styles it, 'a cento;' but it is a very ingenious one. His quotations, which abound in every page, are pertinent; but if he had made more use of his invention and less of his commonplace-book, his work would perhaps have been more valuable than it is. He is generally free from the affected language and ridiculous metaphors which disgrace most of the books of his time.—*Granger's Biographical History*.

BURTON'S ANATOMY OF MELANCHOLY, a book once the favourite of the learned and the witty, and a source of surreptitious learning, though written on a regular plan, consists chiefly of quotations: the author has honestly termed it a cento. He collects, under every division, the opinions of a multitude of writers, without regard to chronological order, and has too often the modesty to decline the interposition of his own sentiments. Indeed the bulk of his materials generally overwhelms him. In the course of his folio he has contrived to treat a great variety of topics, that seem very loosely connected with the general subject; and, like Bayle, when he starts a favourite train of quotations, he does not scruple to let the digression outrun the principal question. Thus, from the doctrines of religion to military discipline, from inland navigation to the morality of dancing-schools, every thing is discussed and determined.—*Ferriar's Illustrations of Sterne*, p. 58.

The archness which BURTON displays occasionally, and his indulgence of playful digressions from the most serious discussions, often give his style an air of familiar conversation, notwithstanding the laborious collections which supply his text. He was capable of writing excellent poetry, but he seems to have cultivated this talent too little. The English verses prefixed to his book, which possess beautiful imagery, and great sweetness of versification, have been frequently published. His Latin elegiac verses addressed to his book, shew a very agreeable turn for raillery.—*Ibid.* p. 58.

When the force of the subject opens his own vein of prose, we discover valuable sense and brilliant expression. Such is his account of the first feelings of melancholy persons, written, probably, from his own experience. [See p. 154, of the present edition.]—*Ibid.* p. 60.

During a pedantic age, like that in which BURTON'S production appeared, it must have been eminently serviceable to writers of many descriptions. Hence the unlearned might furnish themselves with appropriate scraps of Greek and Latin, whilst men of letters would find their enquiries shortened, by knowing where they might look for what both ancients and moderns had advanced on the subject of human passions. I confess my inability to point out any other English author who has so largely dealt in apt and original quotation.—*Manuscript note of the late George Steevens, Esq., in his copy of* THE ANATOMY OF MELANCHOLY.

DEMOCRITUS JUNIOR AD LIBRUM SUUM.

Vade liber, qualis, non ausum dicere, felix,

Te nisi felicem fecerit Alma dies.

Vade tamen quocunque lubet, quascunque per oras,

Et Genium Domini fac imitere tui.

I blandas inter Charites, mystamque saluta

Musarum quemvis, si tibi lector erit.

Rura colas, urbem, subeasve palatia regum,

Submisse, placide, te sine dente geras.

Nobilis, aut si quis te forte inspexerit heros,

Da te morigerum, perlegat usque lubet.

Est quod Nobilitas, est quod desideret heros,

Gratior haec forsan charta placere potest.

Si quis morosus Cato, tetricusque Senator,

Hunc etiam librum forte videre velit,

Sive magistratus, tum te reverenter habeto;

Sed nullus; muscas non capiunt Aquilae.

Non vacat his tempus fugitivum impendere nugis,

Nec tales cupio; par mihi lector erit.

Si matrona gravis casu diverterit istuc,

Illustris domina, aut te Comitissa legat:

Est quod displiceat, placeat quod forsitan illis,

Ingerere his noli te modo, pande tamen.

At si virgo tuas dignabitur inclyta chartas

Tangere, sive schedis haereat illa tuis:

Da modo te facilem, et quaedam folia esse memento

Conveniant oculis quae magis apta suis.

Si generosa ancilla tuos aut alma puella

Visura est ludos, annue, pande lubens.

Dic utinam nunc ipse meus *[6]*(nam diligit istas)

In praesens esset conspiciendus herus.

Ignotus notusve mihi de gente togata

Sive aget in ludis, pulpita sive colet,

Sive in Lycaeo, et nugas evolverit istas,

Si quasdam mendas viderit inspiciens,

Da veniam Authori, dices; nam plurima vellet

Expungi, quae jam displicuisse sciat.

Sive Melancholicus quisquam, seu blandus Amator,

Aulicus aut Civis, seu bene comptus eques

Huc appellat, age et tuto te crede legenti,

Multa istic forsan non male nata leget.

Quod fugiat, caveat, quodque amplexabitur, ista

Pagina fortassis promere multa potest.

At si quis Medicus coram te sistet, amice

Fac circumspecte, et te sine labe geras:

Inveniet namque ipse meis quoque plurima scriptis,

Non leve subsidium quae sibi forsan erunt.

Si quis Causidicus chartas impingat in istas,

Nil mihi vobiscum, pessima turba vale;

Sit nisi vir bonus, et juris sine fraude peritus,

Tum legat, et forsan doctior inde siet.

Si quis cordatus, facilis, lectorque benignus

Huc oculos vertat, quae velit ipse legat;

Candidus ignoscet, metuas nil, pande libenter,

Offensus mendis non erit ille tuis,

Laudabit nonnulla. Venit si Rhetor ineptus,

Limata et tersa, et qui bene cocta petit,

Claude citus librum; nulla hic nisi ferrea verba,

Offendent stomachum quae minus apta suum.

At si quis non eximius de plebe poeta,

Annue; namque istic plurima ficta leget.

Nos sumus e numero, nullus mihi spirat Apollo,

Grandiloquus Vates quilibet esse nequit.

Si Criticus Lector, tumidus Censorque molestus,

Zoilus et Momus, si rabiosa cohors:

Ringe, freme, et noli tum pandere, turba malignis

Si occurrat sannis invidiosa suis:

Fac fugias; si nulla tibi sit copia eundi,

Contemnes, tacite scommata quaeque feres.

Frendeat, allatret, vacuas gannitibus auras

Impleat, haud cures; his placuisse nefas.

Verum age si forsan divertat purior hospes,

Cuique sales, ludi, displiceantque joci,

Objiciatque tibi sordes, lascivaque: dices,

Lasciva est Domino et Musa jocosa tuo,

Nec lasciva tamen, si pensitet omne; sed esto;

Sit lasciva licet pagina, vita proba est.

Barbarus, indoctusque rudis spectator in istam

Si messem intrudat, fuste fugabis eum,

Fungum pelle procul (jubeo) nam quid mihi fungo?

Conveniunt stomacho non minus ista suo.

Sed nec pelle tamen; laeto omnes accipe vultu,

Quos, quas, vel quales, inde vel unde viros.

Gratus erit quicunque venit, gratissimus hospes

Quisquis erit, facilis difficilisque mihi.

Nam si culparit, quaedam culpasse juvabit,

Culpando faciet me meliora sequi.

Sed si laudarit, neque laudibus efferar ullis,

Sit satis hisce malis opposuisse bonum.

Haec sunt quae nostro placuit mandare libello,

Et quae dimittens dicere jussit Herus.

DEMOCRITUS JUNIOR TO HIS BOOK

PARAPHRASTIC METRICAL TRANSLATION.

Go forth my book into the open day;

Happy, if made so by its garish eye.

O'er earth's wide surface take thy vagrant way,

To imitate thy master's genius try.

The Graces three, the Muses nine salute,

Should those who love them try to con thy lore.

The country, city seek, grand thrones to boot,

With gentle courtesy humbly bow before.

Should nobles gallant, soldiers frank and brave

Seek thy acquaintance, hail their first advance:

From twitch of care thy pleasant vein may save,

May laughter cause or wisdom give perchance.

Some surly Cato, Senator austere,

Haply may wish to peep into thy book:

Seem very nothing—tremble and revere:

No forceful eagles, butterflies e'er look.

They love not thee: of them then little seek,

And wish for readers triflers like thyself.

Of ludeful matron watchful catch the beck,

Or gorgeous countess full of pride and pelf.

They may say pish! and frown, and yet read on:

Cry odd, and silly, coarse, and yet amusing.

Should dainty damsels seek thy page to con,

Spread thy best stores: to them be ne'er refusing:

Say, fair one, master loves thee dear as life;

Would he were here to gaze on thy sweet look.

Should known or unknown student, freed from strife

Of logic and the schools, explore my book:

Cry mercy critic, and thy book withhold:

Be some few errors pardon'd though observ'd:

An humble author to implore makes bold.

Thy kind indulgence, even undeserv'd,

Should melancholy wight or pensive lover,

Courtier, snug cit, or carpet knight so trim

Our blossoms cull, he'll find himself in clover,

Gain sense from precept, laughter from our whim.

Should learned leech with solemn air unfold

Thy leaves, beware, be civil, and be wise:

Thy volume many precepts sage may hold,

His well fraught head may find no trifling prize.

Should crafty lawyer trespass on our ground,

Caitiffs avaunt! disturbing tribe away!

Unless (white crow) an honest one be found;

He'll better, wiser go for what we say.

Should some ripe scholar, gentle and benign,

With candour, care, and judgment thee peruse:

Thy faults to kind oblivion he'll consign;

Nor to thy merit will his praise refuse.

Thou may'st be searched for polish'd words and verse

By flippant spouter, emptiest of praters:

Tell him to seek them in some mawkish verse:

My periods all are rough as nutmeg graters.

The doggerel poet, wishing thee to read,

Reject not; let him glean thy jests and stories.

His brother I, of lowly sembling breed:

Apollo grants to few Parnassian glories.

Menac'd by critic with sour furrowed brow,

Momus or Troilus or Scotch reviewer:

Ruffle your heckle, grin and growl and vow:

Ill-natured foes you thus will find the fewer,

When foul-mouth'd senseless railers cry thee down,

Reply not: fly, and show the rogues thy stern;

They are not worthy even of a frown:

Good taste or breeding they can never learn;

Or let them clamour, turn a callous ear,

As though in dread of some harsh donkey's bray.

If chid by censor, friendly though severe,

To such explain and turn thee not away.

Thy vein, says he perchance, is all too free;

Thy smutty language suits not learned pen:

Reply, Good Sir, throughout, the context see;

Thought chastens thought; so prithee judge again.

Besides, although my master's pen may wander

Through devious paths, by which it ought not stray,

His life is pure, beyond the breath of slander:

So pardon grant; 'tis merely but his way.

Some rugged ruffian makes a hideous rout—

Brandish thy cudgel, threaten him to baste;

The filthy fungus far from thee cast out;

Such noxious banquets never suit my taste.

Yet, calm and cautious moderate thy ire,

Be ever courteous should the case allow—

Sweet malt is ever made by gentle fire:

Warm to thy friends, give all a civil bow.

Even censure sometimes teaches to improve,

Slight frosts have often cured too rank a crop,

So, candid blame my spleen shall never move,

For skilful gard'ners wayward branches lop.

Go then, my book, and bear my words in mind;

Guides safe at once, and pleasant them you'll find.

THE ARGUMENT OF THE FRONTISPIECE.

Ten distinct Squares here seen apart,

Are joined in one by Cutter's art.

I.
Old Democritus under a tree,

Sits on a stone with book on knee;

About him hang there many features,

Of Cats, Dogs and such like creatures,

Of which he makes anatomy,

The seat of black choler to see.

Over his head appears the sky,

And Saturn Lord of melancholy.

II.
To the left a landscape of Jealousy,

Presents itself unto thine eye.

A Kingfisher, a Swan, an Hern,

Two fighting-cocks you may discern,

Two roaring Bulls each other hie,

To assault concerning venery.

Symbols are these; I say no more,

Conceive the rest by that's afore.

III.
The next of solitariness,

A portraiture doth well express,

By sleeping dog, cat: Buck and Doe,

Hares, Conies in the desert go:

Bats, Owls the shady bowers over,

In melancholy darkness hover.

Mark well: If't be not as't should be,

Blame the bad Cutter, and not me.

IV.
I'th' under column there doth stand

Inamorato with folded hand;

Down hangs his head, terse and polite,

Some ditty sure he doth indite.

His lute and books about him lie,

As symptoms of his vanity.

If this do not enough disclose,

To paint him, take thyself by th' nose.

V.
Hypocondriacus leans on his arm,

Wind in his side doth him much harm,

And troubles him full sore, God knows,

Much pain he hath and many woes.

About him pots and glasses lie,

Newly brought from's Apothecary.

This Saturn's aspects signify,

You see them portray'd in the sky.

VI.
Beneath them kneeling on his knee,

A superstitious man you see:

He fasts, prays, on his Idol fixt,

Tormented hope and fear betwixt:

For Hell perhaps he takes more pain,

Than thou dost Heaven itself to gain.

Alas poor soul, I pity thee,

What stars incline thee so to be?

VII.
But see the madman rage downright

With furious looks, a ghastly sight.

Naked in chains bound doth he lie,

And roars amain he knows not why!

Observe him; for as in a glass,

Thine angry portraiture it was.

His picture keeps still in thy presence;

'Twixt him and thee, there's no difference.

VIII, IX.
Borage and *Hellebor* fill two scenes,

Sovereign plants to purge the veins

Of melancholy, and cheer the heart,

Of those black fumes which make it smart;

To clear the brain of misty fogs,

Which dull our senses, and Soul clogs.

The best medicine that e'er God made

For this malady, if well assay'd.

X.
Now last of all to fill a place,

Presented is the Author's face;

And in that habit which he wears,

His image to the world appears.

His mind no art can well express,

That by his writings you may guess.

It was not pride, nor yet vainglory,

(Though others do it commonly)

Made him do this: if you must know,

The Printer would needs have it so.

Then do not frown or scoff at it,

Deride not, or detract a whit.

For surely as thou dost by him,

He will do the same again.

Then look upon't, behold and see,

As thou lik'st it, so it likes thee.

And I for it will stand in view,

Thine to command, Reader, adieu.

THE AUTHOR'S ABSTRACT OF MELANCHOLY, Διαλογῶς
When I go musing all alone

Thinking of divers things fore-known.

When I build castles in the air,

Void of sorrow and void of fear,

Pleasing myself with phantasms sweet,

Methinks the time runs very fleet.

All my joys to this are folly,

Naught so sweet as melancholy.

When I lie waking all alone,

Recounting what I have ill done,

My thoughts on me then tyrannise,

Fear and sorrow me surprise,

Whether I tarry still or go,

Methinks the time moves very slow.

All my griefs to this are jolly,

Naught so mad as melancholy.

When to myself I act and smile,

With pleasing thoughts the time beguile,

By a brook side or wood so green,

Unheard, unsought for, or unseen,

A thousand pleasures do me bless,

And crown my soul with happiness.

All my joys besides are folly,

None so sweet as melancholy.

When I lie, sit, or walk alone,

I sigh, I grieve, making great moan,

In a dark grove, or irksome den,

With discontents and Furies then,

A thousand miseries at once

Mine heavy heart and soul ensconce,

All my griefs to this are jolly,

None so sour as melancholy.

Methinks I hear, methinks I see,

Sweet music, wondrous melody,

Towns, palaces, and cities fine;

Here now, then there; the world is mine,

Rare beauties, gallant ladies shine,

Whate'er is lovely or divine.

All other joys to this are folly,

None so sweet as melancholy.

Methinks I hear, methinks I see

Ghosts, goblins, fiends; my phantasy

Presents a thousand ugly shapes,

Headless bears, black men, and apes,

Doleful outcries, and fearful sights,

My sad and dismal soul affrights.

All my griefs to this are jolly,

None so damn'd as melancholy.

Methinks I court, methinks I kiss,

Methinks I now embrace my mistress.

O blessed days, O sweet content,

In Paradise my time is spent.

Such thoughts may still my fancy move,

So may I ever be in love.

All my joys to this are folly,

Naught so sweet as melancholy.

When I recount love's many frights,

My sighs and tears, my waking nights,

My jealous fits; O mine hard fate

I now repent, but 'tis too late.

No torment is so bad as love,

So bitter to my soul can prove.

All my griefs to this are jolly,

Naught so harsh as melancholy.

Friends and companions get you gone,

'Tis my desire to be alone;

Ne'er well but when my thoughts and I

Do domineer in privacy.

No Gem, no treasure like to this,

'Tis my delight, my crown, my bliss.

All my joys to this are folly,

Naught so sweet as melancholy.

'Tis my sole plague to be alone,

I am a beast, a monster grown,

I will no light nor company,

I find it now my misery.

The scene is turn'd, my joys are gone,

Fear, discontent, and sorrows come.

All my griefs to this are jolly,

Naught so fierce as melancholy.

I'll not change life with any king,

I ravisht am: can the world bring

More joy, than still to laugh and smile,

In pleasant toys time to beguile?

Do not, O do not trouble me,

So sweet content I feel and see.

All my joys to this are folly,

None so divine as melancholy.

I'll change my state with any wretch,

Thou canst from gaol or dunghill fetch;

My pain's past cure, another hell,

I may not in this torment dwell!

Now desperate I hate my life,

Lend me a halter or a knife;

All my griefs to this are jolly,

Naught so damn'd as melancholy.

DEMOCRITUS JUNIOR TO THE READER.

Gentle reader, I presume thou wilt be very inquisitive to know what antic or personate actor this is, that so insolently intrudes upon this common theatre, to the world's view, arrogating another man's name; whence he is, why he doth it, and what he hath to say; although, as *[7]he* said, *Primum si noluero, non respondebo, quis coacturus est?* I am a free man born, and may choose whether I will tell; who can compel me? If I be

urged, I will as readily reply as that Egyptian in *[8]*Plutarch, when a curious fellow would needs know what he had in his basket, *Quum vides velatam, quid inquiris in rem absconditam?* It was therefore covered, because he should not know what was in it. Seek not after that which is hid; if the contents please thee, *[9]*and be for thy use, suppose the Man in the Moon, or whom thou wilt to be the author; I would not willingly be known. Yet in some sort to give thee satisfaction, which is more than I need, I will show a reason, both of this usurped name, title, and subject. And first of the name of Democritus; lest any man, by reason of it, should be deceived, expecting a pasquil, a satire, some ridiculous treatise (as I myself should have done), some prodigious tenet, or paradox of the earth's motion, of infinite worlds, *in infinito vacuo, ex fortuita atomorum collisione*, in an infinite waste, so caused by an accidental collision of motes in the sun, all which Democritus held, Epicurus and their master Lucippus of old maintained, and are lately revived by Copernicus, Brunus, and some others. Besides, it hath been always an ordinary custom, as *[10]*Gellius observes, for later writers and impostors, to broach many absurd and insolent fictions, under the name of so noble a philosopher as Democritus, to get themselves credit, and by that means the more to be respected, as artificers usually do, *Novo qui marmori ascribunt Praxatilem suo.* 'Tis not so with me.
*[11]*Non hic Centaurus, non Gorgonas, Harpyasque

Invenies, hominem pagina nostra sapit.

No Centaurs here, or Gorgons look to find,

My subject is of man and human kind.

Thou thyself art the subject of my discourse.
*[12]*Quicquid agunt homines, votum, timor, ira, voluptas,

Gaudia, discursus, nostri farrago libelli.

Whate'er men do, vows, fears, in ire, in sport,

Joys, wand'rings, are the sum of my report.

My intent is no otherwise to use his name, than Mercurius Gallobelgicus, Mercurius Britannicus, use the name of Mercury, *[13]*Democritus Christianus, &c.; although there be some other circumstances for which I have masked myself under this vizard, and some peculiar respect which I cannot so well express, until I have set down a brief character of this our Democritus, what he was, with an epitome of his life.
Democritus, as he is described by *[14]*Hippocrates and *[15]*Laertius, was a little wearish old man, very melancholy by nature, averse from company in his latter days, *[16]*and much given to solitariness, a famous philosopher in his age, *[17]*coaevus with Socrates, wholly addicted to his studies at the last, and to a private life: wrote many excellent works, a great divine, according to the divinity of those times, an expert physician,

a politician, an excellent mathematician, as *[18]*Diacosmus and the rest
of his works do witness. He was much delighted with the studies of
husbandry, saith *[19]*Columella, and often I find him cited
by *[20]*Constantinus and others treating of that subject. He knew the
natures, differences of all beasts, plants, fishes, birds; and, as some say,
could *[21]*understand the tunes and voices of them. In a word, he
was *omnifariam doctus*, a general scholar, a great student; and to the
intent he might better contemplate, *[22]*I find it related by some, that he
put out his eyes, and was in his old age voluntarily blind, yet saw more
than all Greece besides, and *[23]* writ of every subject, *Nihil in toto opificio
naturae, de quo non scripsit. [24]*A man of an excellent wit, profound
conceit; and to attain knowledge the better in his younger years, he
travelled to Egypt and *[25]* Athens, to confer with learned
men, *[26]*admired of some, despised of others. After a wandering life, he
settled at Abdera, a town in Thrace, and was sent for thither to be their
lawmaker, recorder, or town-clerk, as some will; or as others, he was
there bred and born. Howsoever it was, there he lived at last in a garden
in the suburbs, wholly betaking himself to his studies and a private
life, *[27]*saving that sometimes he would walk down to the haven,*[28]*and
laugh heartily at such variety of ridiculous objects, which there he
saw. Such a one was Democritus.

But in the mean time, how doth this concern me, or upon what reference
do I usurp his habit? I confess, indeed, that to compare myself unto him
for aught I have yet said, were both impudency and arrogancy. I do not
presume to make any parallel, *Antistat mihi millibus trecentis, [29]parvus
sum, nullus sum, altum nec spiro, nec spero.* Yet thus much I will say of
myself, and that I hope without all suspicion of pride, or self-conceit, I
have lived a silent, sedentary, solitary, private life, *mihi et musis* in the
University, as long almost as Xenocrates in Athens, *ad senectam fere* to
learn wisdom as he did, penned up most part in my study. For I have
been brought up a student in the most flourishing college of
Europe, *[30] augustissimo collegio*, and can brag with *[31]*Jovius,
almost, *in ea luce domicilii Vacicani, totius orbis celeberrimi, per 37 annos
multa opportunaque didici*; for thirty years I have continued (having the
use of as good *[32]*libraries as ever he had) a scholar, and would be
therefore loath, either by living as a drone, to be an unprofitable or
unworthy member of so learned and noble a society, or to write that
which should be any way dishonourable to such a royal and ample
foundation. Something I have done, though by my profession a divine,
yet *turbine raptus ingenii*, as *[33]*he said, out of a running wit, an
unconstant, unsettled mind, I had a great desire (not able to attain to a
superficial skill in any) to have some smattering in all, to be *aliquis in
omnibus, nullus in singulis, [34]* which *[35]*Plato commends, out of
him *[36]*Lipsius approves and furthers, as fit to be imprinted in all
curious wits, not to be a slave of one science, or dwell altogether in one
subject, as most do, but to rove abroad, *centum puer artium*, to have an
oar in every man's boat, to *[37]* taste of every dish, and sip of every
cup, which, saith *[38]*Montaigne, was well performed by Aristotle, and his
learned countryman Adrian Turnebus. This roving humour (though not
with like success) I have ever had, and like a ranging spaniel, that barks

at every bird he sees, leaving his game, I have followed all, saving that
which I should, and may justly complain, and truly, *qui ubique est,
nusquam est, [39]*which *[40]*Gesner did in modesty, that I have read many
books, but to little purpose, for want of good method; I have confusedly
tumbled over divers authors in our libraries, with small profit, for want of
art, order, memory, judgment. I never travelled but in map or card, in
which mine unconfined thoughts have freely expatiated, as having ever
been especially delighted with the study of Cosmography. *[41]*Saturn was
lord of my geniture, culminating, &c., and Mars principal significator of
manners, in partile conjunction with my ascendant; both fortunate in
their houses, &c. I am not poor, I am not rich; *nihil est, nihil deest*, I have
little, I want nothing: all my treasure is in Minerva's tower. Greater
preferment as I could never get, so am I not in debt for it, I have a
competence (*laus Deo*) from my noble and munificent patrons, though I
live still a collegiate student, as Democritus in his garden, and lead a
monastic life, *ipse mihi theatrum*, sequestered from those tumults and
troubles of the world, *Et tanquam in specula positus*, (*[42]*as he said) in
some high place above you all, like Stoicus Sapiens, *omnia saecula,
praeterita presentiaque videns, uno velut intuitu*, I hear and see what is
done abroad, how others *[43]*run, ride, turmoil, and macerate themselves
in court and country, far from those wrangling lawsuits, *aulia vanitatem,
fori ambitionem, ridere mecum soleo*: I laugh at all, *[44]*only secure, lest
my suit go amiss, my ships perish, corn and cattle miscarry, trade decay,
I have no wife nor children good or bad to provide for. A mere spectator of
other men's fortunes and adventures, and how they act their parts,
which methinks are diversely presented unto me, as from a common
theatre or scene. I hear new news every day, and those ordinary rumours
of war, plagues, fires, inundations, thefts, murders, massacres, meteors,
comets, spectrums, prodigies, apparitions, of towns taken, cities besieged
in France, Germany, Turkey, Persia, Poland, &c., daily musters and
preparations, and such like, which these tempestuous times afford,
battles fought, so many men slain, monomachies, shipwrecks, piracies
and sea-fights; peace, leagues, stratagems, and fresh alarms. A vast
confusion of vows, wishes, actions, edicts, petitions, lawsuits, pleas,
laws, proclamations, complaints, grievances are daily brought to our
ears. New books every day, pamphlets, corantoes, stories, whole
catalogues of volumes of all sorts, new paradoxes, opinions, schisms,
heresies, controversies in philosophy, religion, &c. Now come tidings of
weddings, maskings, mummeries, entertainments, jubilees, embassies,
tilts and tournaments, trophies, triumphs, revels, sports, plays: then
again, as in a new shifted scene, treasons, cheating tricks, robberies,
enormous villainies in all kinds, funerals, burials, deaths of princes, new
discoveries, expeditions, now comical, then tragical matters. Today we
hear of new lords and officers created, tomorrow of some great men
deposed, and then again of fresh honours conferred; one is let loose,
another imprisoned; one purchaseth, another breaketh: he thrives, his
neighbour turns bankrupt; now plenty, then again dearth and famine;
one runs, another rides, wrangles, laughs, weeps, &c. This I daily hear,
and such like, both private and public news, amidst the gallantry and
misery of the world; jollity, pride, perplexities and cares, simplicity and

villainy; subtlety, knavery, candour and integrity, mutually mixed and offering themselves; I rub on *privus privatus*; as I have still lived, so I now continue, *statu quo prius*, left to a solitary life, and mine own domestic discontents: saving that sometimes, *ne quid mentiar*, as Diogenes went into the city, and Democritus to the haven to see fashions, I did for my recreation now and then walk abroad, look into the world, and could not choose but make some little observation, *non tam sagax observator ac simplex recitator*, *[45]* not as they did, to scoff or laugh at all, but with a mixed passion.
*[46]*Bilem saepe, jocum vestri movere tumultus.

Ye wretched mimics, whose fond heats have been,

How oft! the objects of my mirth and spleen.

I did sometime laugh and scoff with Lucian, and satirically tax with Menippus, lament with Heraclitus, sometimes again I was *[47]petulanti splene chachinno*, and then again, *[48]urere bilis jecur*, I was much moved to see that abuse which I could not mend. In which passion howsoever I may sympathise with him or them, 'tis for no such respect I shroud myself under his name; but either in an unknown habit to assume a little more liberty and freedom of speech, or if you will needs know, for that reason and only respect which Hippocrates relates at large in his Epistle to Damegetus, wherein he doth express, how coming to visit him one day, he found Democritus in his garden at Abdera, in the suburbs, *[49]*under a shady bower, *[50]*with a book on his knees, busy at his study, sometimes writing, sometimes walking. The subject of his book was melancholy and madness; about him lay the carcases of many several beasts, newly by him cut up and anatomised; not that he did contemn God's creatures, as he told Hippocrates, but to find out the seat of this *atra bilis*, or melancholy, whence it proceeds, and how it was engendered in men's bodies, to the intent he might better cure it in himself, and by his writings and observation *[51]*teach others how to prevent and avoid it. Which good intent of his, Hippocrates highly commended: Democritus Junior is therefore bold to imitate, and because he left it imperfect, and it is now lost, *quasi succenturiator Democriti*, to revive again, prosecute, and finish in this treatise.

You have had a reason of the name. If the title and inscription offend your gravity, were it a sufficient justification to accuse others, I could produce many sober treatises, even sermons themselves, which in their fronts carry more fantastical names. Howsoever, it is a kind of policy in these days, to prefix a fantastical title to a book which is to be sold; for, as larks come down to a day-net, many vain readers will tarry and stand gazing like silly passengers at an antic picture in a painter's shop, that will not look at a judicious piece. And, indeed, as *[52]*Scaliger observes, nothing more invites a reader than an argument unlooked for, unthought of, and sells better than a scurrile pamphlet, *tum maxime cum novitas excitat [53]palatum*. Many men, saith Gellius, are very conceited in their inscriptions, and able (as [54]Pliny quotes out of Seneca) to make him loiter by the way that went in haste to fetch a midwife for his daughter, now ready to lie down. For my part, I have honourable [55]precedents for this which I have done: I will cite one for all, Anthony Zara, Pap. Epis., his Anatomy of Wit, in four sections, members, subsections, &c., to be read in our libraries.

If any man except against the matter or manner of treating of this my subject, and will demand a reason of it, I can allege more than one; I write of melancholy, by being busy to avoid melancholy. There is no greater cause of melancholy than idleness, no better cure than business, as [56] Rhasis holds: and howbeit, *stultus labor est ineptiarum*, to be busy in toys is to small purpose, yet hear that divine Seneca, *aliud agere quam nihil*, better do to no end, than nothing. I wrote therefore, and busied myself in this playing labour, *oliosaque diligentia ut vitarem torporum feriandi* with Vectius in Macrobius, *atque otium in utile verterem negatium.*

[57]Simul et jucunda et idonea dicere vita,

Lectorem delectando simul atque monendo.

Poets would profit or delight mankind,

And with the pleasing have th' instructive joined.

Profit and pleasure, then, to mix with art,

T' inform the judgment, nor offend the heart,

Shall gain all votes.

To this end I write, like them, saith Lucian, that recite to trees, and declaim to pillars for want of auditors: as [58]Paulus Aegineta ingenuously confesseth, not that anything was unknown or omitted, but to exercise myself, which course if some took, I think it would be good for their bodies, and much better for their souls; or peradventure as others do, for fame, to show myself (*Scire tuum nihil est, nisi te scire hoc sciat alter*). I might be of Thucydides' opinion, [59]to know a thing and not to express it, is all one as if he knew it not. When I first took this task in hand, *et quod ait [60]ille, impellents genio negotium suscepi*, this I aimed at; [61]*vel ut lenirem animum scribendo*, to ease my mind by writing; for I had *gravidum cor, foetum caput*, a kind of imposthume in my head, which I was very desirous to be unladen of, and could imagine no fitter evacuation than this. Besides, I might not well refrain, for *ubi dolor, ibi digitus*, one must needs scratch where it itches. I was not a little offended with this malady, shall I say my mistress Melancholy, my Aegeria, or my *malus genius*? and for that cause, as he that is stung with a scorpion, I would expel *clavum clavo*, [62]comfort one sorrow with another, idleness with idleness, *ut ex vipera Theriacum*, make an antidote out of that which was the prime cause of my disease. Or as he did, of whom *[63]*Felix Plater speaks, that thought he had some of Aristophanes' frogs in his belly, still crying *Breec, okex, coax, coax, oop, oop*, and for that cause studied physic seven years, and travelled over most part of Europe to ease himself. To do myself good I turned over such physicians as our libraries would afford, or my *[64]*private friends impart, and have taken this pains. And why not? Cardan professeth he wrote his book, *De Consolatione* after his son's death, to comfort himself; so did Tully write of the same subject with like intent after his daughter's departure, if it be his at least, or some impostor's put out in his name, which Lipsius probably suspects. Concerning myself, I can peradventure affirm with Marius in Sallust, *[65]*that which others hear or read of, I felt and practised myself; they get their knowledge by books, I mine by melancholising. *Experto crede Roberto.* Something I can speak out of experience, *aerumnabilis experientia me docuit*; and with her in the poet, *[66]Haud ignara mali miseris succurrere disco*; I would help others out of a fellow-feeling; and, as that virtuous lady did of old, *[67]*being a leper herself, bestow all her portion to build an hospital for lepers, I will spend my time and knowledge, which are my greatest fortunes, for the common good of all. Yea, but you will infer that this is *[68]actum agere*, an unnecessary work, *cramben bis coctam apponnere*, the same again and again in other words. To what purpose? *[69]*Nothing is omitted that may well be said, so thought Lucian in the like theme. How many excellent physicians have written just volumes and elaborate tracts of this subject? No news here; that which I have is stolen, from others, *[70]Dicitque mihi mea pagina fur es*. If that severe doom of *[71]*Synesius be true, it is a greater offence to steal dead men's labours, than their clothes, what shall become of most writers? I hold up my hand at the bar among others, and am guilty of felony in this kind, *habes confitentem reum*, I am content to be pressed with the rest. 'Tis most true, *tenet insanabile multos scribendi cacoethes*, and *[72]*there is no end of writing of books, as the wiseman found of old, in this *[73]*scribbling age, especially wherein *[74]*the number of books is without number,(as a worthy man saith,) presses be oppressed, and out of an itching humour that every man hath to show himself, *[75]*desirous of fame and honour (*scribimus indocti doctique*——) he will write no matter what, and scrape together it boots not whence. *[76]*Bewitched with this desire of fame, *etiam mediis in morbis*, to the disparagement of their health, and scarce able to hold a pen, they must say something, *[77]*and get themselves a name, saith Scaliger, though it be to the downfall and ruin of many others. To be counted writers, *scriptores ut salutentur*, to be thought and held polymaths and polyhistors, *apud imperitum vulgus ob ventosae nomen artis*, to get a paper-kingdom: *nulla spe quaestus sed ampla famae*, in this precipitate, ambitious age, *nunc ut est saeculum, inter immaturam eruditionem, ambitiosum et praeceps* ('tis *[78]*Scaliger's censure); and they that are scarce auditors, *vix auditores*, must be masters and teachers, before they be capable and fit hearers. They will rush into all learning, *togatam armatam*, divine, human authors, rake over all indexes and pamphlets for notes, as our merchants do strange havens for traffic, write great tomes, *Cum non sint re vera doctiores, sed loquaciores*, whereas they are not thereby better scholars, but greater praters. They commonly pretend public good, but as *[79]*Gesner observes, 'tis pride and vanity that eggs them on; no news or aught worthy of note, but the same in other terms. *Ne feriarentur fortasse typographi vel ideo scribendum est aliquid ut se vixisse testentur.* As apothecaries we make new mixtures everyday, pour out of one vessel into another; and as those old Romans robbed all the cities of the world, to set out their bad-sited Rome, we skim off the cream of other men's wits, pick the choice flowers of their tilled gardens to set out our own sterile plots. *Castrant alios ut libros suos per se graciles alieno adipe suffarciant* (so *[80]*Jovius inveighs.) They lard their lean books with the fat of others' works. *Ineruditi fures,* &c. A fault that every writer finds, as I do now, and yet faulty themselves, *[81]Trium literarum homines,* all thieves; they pilfer out of old writers to stuff up their new comments, scrape Ennius' dunghills, and out of *[82]*Democritus' pit, as I have done. By which means it comes to pass, *[83]*that not only libraries and shops are full of our putrid papers, but every close-stool and jakes, *Scribunt carmina quae legunt cacantes;* they serve to put under pies, to *[84]*lap spice in, and keep roast meat from burning. With us in France, saith *[85]*Scaliger, every man hath liberty to write, but few ability. *[86]*Heretofore learning was graced by judicious scholars, but now noble sciences are vilified by base and illiterate scribblers, that either write for vainglory, need, to get money, or as Parasites to flatter and collogue with some great men, they put cut *[87]burras, quisquiliasque ineptiasque. [88]*Amongst so many thousand authors you shall scarce find one, by reading of whom you shall be any whit better, but rather much worse, *quibus inficitur potius, quam perficitur,* by which he is rather infected than any way perfected. *[89]*————Qui talia legit,

Quid didicit tandem, quid scit nisi somnia, nugas?

So that oftentimes it falls out (which Callimachus taxed of old) a great book is a great mischief. *[90]*Cardan finds fault with Frenchmen and Germans, for their scribbling to no purpose, *non inquit ab edendo deterreo, modo novum aliquid inveniant,* he doth not bar them to write, so that it be some new invention of their own; but we weave the same web still, twist the same rope again and again; or if it be a new invention, 'tis but some bauble or toy which idle fellows write, for as idle fellows to read, and who so cannot invent? *[91]*He must have a barren wit, that in this scribbling age can forge nothing. *[92]*Princes show their armies, rich men vaunt their buildings, soldiers their manhood, and scholars vent their toys; they must read, they must hear whether they will or no.

*[93]*Et quodcunque semel chartis illeverit, omnes

Gestiet a furno redeuntes scire lacuque,

Et pueros et anus————

What once is said and writ, all men must know,

Old wives and children as they come and go.

What a company of poets hath this year brought out, as Pliny complains
to Sossius Sinesius. *[94]*This April every day some or other have
recited. What a catalogue of new books all this year, all this age (I say),
have our Frankfort Marts, our domestic Marts brought out? Twice a
year, *[95]* *Proferunt se nova ingenia et ostentant*, we stretch our wits out,
and set them to sale, *magno conatu nihil agimus*. So that
which *[96]*Gesner much desires, if a speedy reformation be not had, by
some prince's edicts and grave supervisors, to restrain this liberty, it will
run on in *infinitum.Quis tam avidus librorum helluo*, who can read them?
As already, we shall have a vast chaos and confusion of books, we
are *[97]*oppressed with them, *[98]*our eyes ache with reading, our fingers
with turning. For my part I am one of the number, *nos numerus sumus*,
(we are mere ciphers): I do not deny it, I have only this of Macrobius to
say for myself, *Omne meum, nihil meum*, 'tis all mine, and none mine. As
a good housewife out of divers fleeces weaves one piece of cloth, a bee
gathers wax and honey out of many flowers, and makes a new bundle of
all, *Floriferis ut apes in saltibus omnia libant*, I have
laboriously *[99]*collected this cento out of divers writers, and that *sine
injuria*, I have wronged no authors, but given every man his own;
which *[100]*Hierom so much commends in Nepotian; he stole not whole
verses, pages, tracts, as some do nowadays, concealing their authors'
names, but still said this was Cyprian's, that Lactantius, that Hilarius,
so said Minutius Felix, so Victorinus, thus far Arnobius: I cite and quote
mine authors (which, howsoever some illiterate scribblers account
pedantical, as a cloak of ignorance, and opposite to their affected fine
style, I must and will use) *sumpsi, non suripui*; and what Varro, *lib. 6. de
re rust.* speaks of bees, *minime maleficae nullius opus vellicantes faciunt
delerius*, I can say of myself, Whom have I injured? The matter is theirs
most part, and yet mine, *apparet unde sumptum sit* (which Seneca
approves), *aliud tamen quam unde sumptum sit apparet*, which nature
doth with the aliment of our bodies incorporate, digest, assimilate, I
do *concoquere quod hausi*, dispose of what I take. I make them pay
tribute, to set out this my Maceronicon, the method only is mine own, I
must usurp that of *[101]*Wecker *e Ter. nihil dictum quod non dictum prius,
methodus sola artificem ostendit*, we can say nothing but what hath been
said, the composition and method is ours only, and shows a scholar.
Oribasius, Aesius, Avicenna, have all out of Galen, but to their own
method, *diverso stilo, non diversa fide*. Our poets steal from Homer; he
spews, saith Aelian, they lick it up. Divines use Austin's words verbatim
still, and our story-dressers do as much; he that comes last is commonly

best,

————donec quid grandius aetas

Postera sorsque ferat melior.————*[102]*

Though there were many giants of old in physic and philosophy, yet I say with *[103]*Didacus Stella, A dwarf standing on the shoulders of a giant may see farther than a giant himself; I may likely add, alter, and see farther than my predecessors; and it is no greater prejudice for me to indite after others, than for Aelianus Montaltus, that famous physician, to write *de morbis capitis*after Jason Pratensis, Heurnius, Hildesheim, &c., many horses to run in a race, one logician, one rhetorician, after another. Oppose then what thou wilt,

Allatres licet usque nos et usque

Et gannitibus improbis lacessas.

I solve it thus. And for those other faults of barbarism, *[104]*Doric dialect, extemporanean style, tautologies, apish imitation, a rhapsody of rags gathered together from several dunghills, excrements of authors, toys and fopperies confusedly tumbled out, without art, invention, judgment, wit, learning, harsh, raw, rude, fantastical, absurd, insolent, indiscreet, ill-composed, indigested, vain, scurrile, idle, dull, and dry; I confess all ('tis partly affected), thou canst not think worse of me than I do of myself. 'Tis not worth the reading, I yield it, I desire thee not to lose time in perusing so vain a subject, I should be peradventure loath myself to read him or thee so writing; 'tis not *operae, pretium.* All I say is this, that I have *[105]*precedents for it, which Isocrates calls *perfugium iis qui peccant,* others as absurd, vain, idle, illiterate, &c. *Nonnulli alii idem fecerunt*; others have done as much, it may be more, and perhaps thou thyself, *Novimus et qui te,* &c. We have all our faults; *scimus, et hanc, veniaim,* &c.; *[106]*thou censurest me, so have I done others, and may do thee, *Cedimus inque vicem,* &c., 'tis *lex talionis, quid pro quo.* Go now, censure, criticise, scoff, and rail.

*[107]*Nasutus cis usque licet, sis denique nasus:

Non potes in nugas dicere plura meas,

Ipse ego quam dixi, &c.

Wert thou all scoffs and flouts, a very Momus,

Than we ourselves, thou canst not say worse of us.

Thus, as when women scold, have I cried whore first, and in some men's censures I am afraid I have overshot myself, *Laudare se vani, vituperare stulti*, as I do not arrogate, I will not derogate. *Primus vestrum non sum, nec imus*, I am none of the best, I am none of the meanest of you. As I am an inch, or so many feet, so many parasangs, after him or him, I may be peradventure an ace before thee. Be it therefore as it is, well or ill, I have essayed, put myself upon the stage; I must abide the censure, I may not escape it. It is most true, *stylus virum arguit*, our style bewrays us, and as *[108]*hunters find their game by the trace, so is a man's genius descried by his works, *Multo melius ex sermone quam lineamentis, de moribus hominum judicamus*; it was old Cato's rule. I have laid myself open (I know it) in this treatise, turned mine inside outward: I shall be censured, I doubt not; for, to say truth with Erasmus, *nihil morosius hominum judiciis*, there is nought so peevish as men's judgments; yet this is some comfort, *ut palata, sic judicia*, our censures are as various as our palates.
*[109]*Tres mihi convivae prope dissentire videntur,

Poscentes vario multum diversa palato, &c.

Three guests I have, dissenting at my feast,

Requiring each to gratify his taste

With different food.

Our writings are as so many dishes, our readers guests, our books like beauty, that which one admires another rejects; so are we approved as men's fancies are inclined. *Pro captu lectoris habent sua fata libelli.*. That which is most pleasing to one is *amaracum sui*, most harsh to another. *Quot homines, tot sententiae*, so many men, so many minds: that which thou condemnest he commends. *[110]*Quod petis, id sane est invisum acidumque duobus. He respects matter, thou art wholly for words; he loves a loose and free style, thou art all for neat composition, strong lines, hyperboles, allegories; he desires a fine frontispiece, enticing pictures, such as *[111]*Hieron. Natali the Jesuit hath cut to the Dominicals, to draw on the reader's attention, which thou rejectest; that which one admires, another explodes as most absurd and ridiculous. If it be not point blank to his humour, his method, his conceit, *[112]*si quid, forsan omissum, quod is animo conceperit, si quae dictio, &c.* If aught be omitted, or added, which he likes, or dislikes, thou art *mancipium paucae lectionis*, an idiot, an ass, *nullus es*, or *plagiarius*, a trifler, a trivant, thou art an idle fellow; or else it is a thing of mere industry, a collection without wit or invention, a very toy. *[113]*Facilia sic putant omnes quae jam facta, nec de salebris cogitant, ubi via strata; so men are valued, their labours vilified by fellows of no worth themselves, as things of nought, who could not have done as much. *Unusquisque abundat sensu suo*, every man abounds in his own sense; and whilst each particular party is so affected, how should one please all?
*[114]*Quid dem? quid non dem? Renuis tu quod jubet ille.

————What courses must I choose?

What not? What both would order you refuse.

How shall I hope to express myself to each man's humour and *[115]*conceit, or to give satisfaction to all? Some understand too little, some too much, *qui similiter in legendos libros, atque in salutandos homines irruunt, non cogitantes quales, sed quibus vestibus induti sint,* as *[116]*Austin observes, not regarding what, but who write, *[117]orexin habet auctores celebritas,* not valuing the metal, but stamp that is upon it, *Cantharum aspiciunt, non quid in eo.* If he be not rich, in great place, polite and brave, a great doctor, or full fraught with grand titles, though never so well qualified, he is a dunce; but, as *[118]*Baronius hath it of Cardinal Caraffa's works, he is a mere hog that rejects any man for his poverty. Some are too partial, as friends to overween, others come with a prejudice to carp, vilify, detract, and scoff; (*qui de me forsan, quicquid est, omni contemptu contemptius judicant*) some as bees for honey, some as spiders to gather poison. What shall I do in this case? As a Dutch host, if you come to an inn in. Germany, and dislike your fare, diet, lodging, &c., replies in a surly tone, *[119]aliud tibi quaeras diversorium,* if you like not this, get you to another inn: I resolve, if you like not my writing, go read something else. I do not much esteem thy censure, take thy course, it is not as thou wilt, nor as I will, but when we have both done, that of *[120]*Plinius Secundus to Trajan will prove true, Every man's witty labour takes not, except the matter, subject, occasion, and some commending favourite happen to it. If I be taxed, exploded by thee and some such, I shall haply be approved and commended by others, and so have been (*Expertus loquor*), and may truly say with *[121]*Jovius in like case, *(absit verbo jactantia) heroum quorundam, pontificum, et virorum nobilium familiaritatem et amicitiam, gratasque gratias, et multorum [122] bene laudatorum laudes sum inde promeritus,* as I have been honoured by some worthy men, so have I been vilified by others, and shall be. At the first publishing of this book, (which *[123]*Probus of Persius satires), *editum librum continuo mirari homines, atque avide deripere caeperunt,* I may in some sort apply to this my work. The first, second, and third edition were suddenly gone, eagerly read, and, as I have said, not so much approved by some, as scornfully rejected by others. But it was Democritus his fortune, *Idem admirationi et [124]irrisioni habitus.* 'Twas Seneca's fate, that superintendent of wit, learning, judgment, *[125]ad stuporem doctus,* the best of Greek and Latin writers, in Plutarch's opinion; that renowned corrector of vice, as, *[126]*Fabius terms him, and painful omniscious philosopher, that writ so excellently and admirably well, could not please all parties, or escape censure. How is he vilified by *[127]* Caligula, Agellius, Fabius, and Lipsius himself, his chief propugner? *In eo pleraque pernitiosa,* saith the same Fabius, many childish tracts and sentences he hath, *sermo illaboratus,* too negligent often and remiss, as Agellius observes, *oratio vulgaris et protrita, dicaces et ineptae, sententiae, eruditio plebeia,* an homely shallow writer as he is. *In partibus spinas et fastidia habet,* saith *[128]*Lipsius; and, as in all his other works, so especially in his epistles, *aliae in argutiis et ineptiis occupantur, intricatus alicubi, et parum compositus, sine copia rerum hoc fecit,* he jumbles up many things together immethodically, after the Stoics' fashion, *parum ordinavit, multa accumulavit,* &c. If Seneca be thus lashed, and many famous men that I could name, what shall I expect? How shall I that am *vix umbra tanti philosophi* hope to please? No man so absolute (*[129]*Erasmus holds) to satisfy all, except antiquity, prescription, &c., set a bar. But as I have proved in Seneca, this will not always take place, how shall I evade? 'Tis the common doom of all writers, I must (I say) abide it; I seek not applause; *[130]Non ego ventosa venor suffragia plebis*; again, *non sum adeo informis,* I would not be *[131]*vilified:

[132]————laudatus abunde,

Non fastiditus si tibi, lector, ero.

I fear good men's censures, and to their favourable acceptance I submit my labours,

[133]————et linguas mancipiorum

Contemno.————

As the barking of a dog, I securely contemn those malicious and scurrile obloquies, flouts, calumnies of railers and detractors; I scorn the rest. What therefore I have said, *pro tenuitate mea,* I have said.

One or two things yet I was desirous to have amended if I could, concerning the manner of handling this my subject, for which I must apologise, *deprecari,* and upon better advice give the friendly reader notice: it was not mine intent to prostitute my muse in English, or to divulge *secreta Minervae,* but to have exposed this more contract in Latin, if I could have got it printed. Any scurrile pamphlet is welcome to our mercenary stationers in English; they print all
————cuduntque libellos

In quorum foliis vix simia nuda cacaret;

But in Latin they will not deal; which is one of the reasons *[134]*Nicholas Car, in his oration of the paucity of English writers, gives, that so many flourishing wits are smothered in oblivion, lie dead and buried in this our nation. Another main fault is, that I have not revised the copy, and amended the style, which now flows remissly, as it was first conceived; but my leisure would not permit; *Feci nec quod potui, nec quod volui,* I confess it is neither as I would, nor as it should be.

*[135]*Cum relego scripsisse pudet, quia plurima cerno

Me quoque quae fuerant judice digna lini.

When I peruse this tract which I have writ,

I am abash'd, and much I hold unfit.

Et quod gravissimum, in the matter itself, many things I disallow at this present, which when I writ, *[136]Non eadem est aetas, non mens*; I would willingly retract much, &c., but 'tis too late, I can only crave pardon now for what is amiss.

I might indeed, (had I wisely done) observed that precept of the poet, —— —*nonumque prematur in annum,* and have taken more care: or, as Alexander the physician would have done by lapis lazuli, fifty times washed before it be used, I should have revised, corrected and amended this tract; but I had not (as I said) that happy leisure, no amanuenses or assistants. Pancrates in *[137]*Lucian, wanting a servant as he went from Memphis to Coptus in Egypt, took a door bar, and after some superstitious words pronounced (Eucrates the relator was then present) made it stand up like a serving-man, fetch him water, turn the spit, serve in supper, and what work he would besides; and when he had done that service he desired, turned his man to a stick again. I have no such skill to make new men at my pleasure, or means to hire them; no whistle to call like the master of a ship, and bid them run, &c. I have no such authority, no such benefactors, as that noble *[138]*Ambrosius was to Origen, allowing him six or seven amanuenses to write out his dictates; I must for that cause do my business myself, and was therefore enforced, as a bear doth her whelps, to bring forth this confused lump; I had not time to lick it into form, as she doth her young ones, but even so to publish it, as it was first written *quicquid in buccam venit,* in an extemporean style, as *[139]*I do commonly all other exercises, *effudi quicquid dictavit genius meus,* out of a confused company of notes, and writ with as small deliberation as I do ordinarily speak, without all affectation of big words, fustian phrases, jingling terms, tropes, strong lines, that like *[140]*Acesta's arrows caught fire as they flew, strains of wit, brave heats, elegies, hyperbolical exornations, elegancies, &c., which many so much affect. I am *[141]aquae potor,* drink no wine at all, which so much improves our modern wits, a loose, plain, rude writer, *ficum, voco ficum et ligonem ligonem* and as free, as loose, *idem calamo quod in mente, [142]*I call a spade a spade, *animis haec scribo, non auribus,* I respect matter not words; remembering that of Cardan, *verba propter res,* *non res propter verba*: and seeking with Seneca, *quid scribam, non quemadmodum*, rather *what* than *how* to write: for as Philo thinks, *[143]*He that is conversant about matter, neglects words, and those that excel in this art of speaking, have no profound learning, *[144]*Verba nitent phaleris, at nullus verba medullas

Intus habent———

Besides, it was the observation of that wise Seneca, *[145]*when you see a fellow careful about his words, and neat in his speech, know this for a certainty, that man's mind is busied about toys, there's no solidity in him. *Non est ornamentum virile concinnitas*: as he said of a nightingale, — ——*vox es, praeterea nihil*, &c. I am therefore in this point a professed disciple of *[146]*Apollonius a scholar of Socrates, I neglect phrases, and labour wholly to inform my reader's understanding, not to please his ear; 'tis not my study or intent to compose neatly, which an orator requires, but to express myself readily and plainly as it happens. So that as a river runs sometimes precipitate and swift, then dull and slow; now direct, then *per ambages*, now deep, then shallow; now muddy, then clear; now broad, then narrow; doth my style flow: now serious, then light; now comical, then satirical; now more elaborate, then remiss, as the present subject required, or as at that time I was affected. And if thou vouchsafe to read this treatise, it shall seem no otherwise to thee, than the way to an ordinary traveller, sometimes fair, sometimes foul; here champaign, there enclosed; barren, in one place, better soil in another: by woods, groves, hills, dales, plains, &c. I shall lead thee *per ardua montium, et lubrica valllum, et roscida cespitum, et [147]glebosa camporum*, through variety of objects, that which thou shalt like and surely dislike.

For the matter itself or method, if it be faulty, consider I pray you that of *Columella, Nihil perfectum, aut a singulari consummatum industria*, no man can observe all, much is defective no doubt, may be justly taxed, altered, and avoided in Galen, Aristotle, those great masters. *Boni venatoris* (*[148]*one holds) *plures feras capere, non omnes*; he is a good huntsman can catch some, not all: I have done my endeavour. Besides, I dwell not in this study, *Non hic sulcos ducimus, non hoc pulvere desudamus*, I am but a smatterer, I confess, a stranger, *[149]*here and there I pull a flower; I do easily grant, if a rigid censurer should criticise on this which I have writ, he should not find three sole faults, as Scaliger in Terence, but three hundred. So many as he hath done in Cardan's subtleties, as many notable errors as *[150]*Gul Laurembergius, a late professor of Rostock, discovers in that anatomy of Laurentius, or Barocius the Venetian in *Sacro boscus*. And although this be a sixth edition, in which I should have been more accurate, corrected all those former escapes, yet it was *magni laboris opus*, so difficult and tedious, that as carpenters do find out of experience, 'tis much better build a new sometimes, than repair an old house; I could as soon write as much more, as alter that which is written. If aught therefore be amiss (as I grant there is), I require a friendly admonition, no bitter invective, *[151]Sint musis socii Charites, Furia omnis abesto*, otherwise, as in ordinary controversies, *funem contentionis nectamus, sed cui bono*? We may contend, and likely misuse each other, but to what purpose? We are both scholars, say,

[152]———Arcades ambo

Et Cantare pares, et respondere parati.

Both young Arcadians, both alike inspir'd

To sing and answer as the song requir'd.

If we do wrangle, what shall we get by it? Trouble and wrong ourselves, make sport to others. If I be convict of an error, I will yield, I will amend. *Si quid bonis moribus, si quid veritati dissentaneum, in sacris vel humanis literis a me dictum sit, id nec dictum esto.* In the mean time I require a favourable censure of all faults omitted, harsh compositions, pleonasms of words, tautological repetitions (though Seneca bear me out, *nunquam nimis dicitur, quod nunquam satis dicitur*) perturbations of tenses, numbers, printers' faults, &c. My translations are sometimes rather paraphrases than interpretations, *non ad verbum*, but as an author, I use more liberty, and that's only taken which was to my purpose. Quotations are often inserted in the text, which makes the style more harsh, or in the margin, as it happened. Greek authors, Plato, Plutarch, Athenaeus, &c., I have cited out of their interpreters, because the original was not so ready. I have mingled *sacra prophanis*, but I hope not profaned, and in repetition of authors' names, ranked them *per accidens*, not according to chronology; sometimes neoterics before ancients, as my memory suggested. Some things are here altered, expunged in this sixth edition, others amended, much added, because many good *[153]*authors in all kinds are come to my hands since, and 'tis no prejudice, no such indecorum, or oversight.

*[154]*Nunquam ita quicquam bene subducta ratione ad vitam fuit,

Quin res, aetas, usus, semper aliquid apportent novi,

Aliquid moneant, ut illa quae scire te credas, nescias,

Et quae tibi putaris prima, in exercendo ut repudias.

Ne'er was ought yet at first contriv'd so fit,

But use, age, or something would alter it;

Advise thee better, and, upon peruse,

Make thee not say, and what thou tak'st refuse.

But I am now resolved never to put this treatise out again, *Ne quid nimis*, I will not hereafter add, alter, or retract; I have done. The last and greatest exception is, that I, being a divine, have meddled with physic,

[155]Tantumne est ab re tua otii tibi,

Aliena ut cures, eaque nihil quae ad te attinent.

Which Menedemus objected to Chremes; have I so much leisure, or little business of mine own, as to look after other men's matters which concern me not? What have I to do with physic? *Quod medicorum est promittant medici.* The *[156]*Lacedaemonians were once in counsel about state matters, a debauched fellow spake excellent well, and to the purpose, his speech was generally approved: a grave senator steps up, and by all means would have it repealed, though good, because *dehonestabatur pessimo auctore*, it had no better an author; let some good man relate the same, and then it should pass. This counsel was embraced, *factum est*, and it was registered forthwith, *Et sic bona sententia mansit, malus auctor mutatus est.* Thou sayest as much of me, stomachosus as thou art, and grantest, peradventure, this which I have written in physic, not to be amiss, had another done it, a professed physician, or so, but why should I meddle with this tract? Hear me speak. There be many other subjects, I do easily grant, both in humanity and divinity, fit to be treated of, of which had I written *ad ostentationem* only, to show myself, I should have rather chosen, and in which I have been more conversant, I could have more willingly luxuriated, and better satisfied myself and others; but that at this time I was fatally driven upon this rock of melancholy, and carried away by this by-stream, which, as a rillet, is deducted from the main channel of my studies, in which I have pleased and busied myself at idle hours, as a subject most necessary and commodious. Not that I prefer it before divinity, which I do acknowledge to be the queen of professions, and to which all the rest are as handmaids, but that in divinity I saw no such great need. For had I written positively, there be so many books in that kind, so many commentators, treatises, pamphlets, expositions, sermons, that whole teams of oxen cannot draw them; and had I been as forward and ambitious as some others, I might have haply printed a sermon at Paul's Cross, a sermon in St. Marie's Oxon, a sermon in Christ Church, or a sermon before the right honourable, right reverend, a sermon before the right worshipful, a sermon in Latin, in English, a sermon with a name, a sermon without, a sermon, a sermon, &c. But I have been ever as desirous to suppress my labours in this kind, as others have been to press and publish theirs. To have written in controversy had been to cut off an hydra's head, *[157]Lis litem generat*, one begets another, so many duplications, triplications, and swarms of questions. *In sacro bello hoc quod stili mucrone agitur*, that having once begun, I should never make an end. One had much better, as*[158]*Alexander, the sixth pope, long since observed, provoke a great prince than a begging friar, a Jesuit, or a seminary priest, I will add, for *inexpugnabile genus hoc hominum*, they are an irrefragable society, they must and will have the last word; and that with such eagerness, impudence, abominable lying, falsifying, and bitterness in their questions they proceed, that as he *[159]*said, *furorne caecus, an rapit vis acrior, an culpa, responsum date?* Blind fury, or error, or rashness, or what it is that eggs them, I know not, I am sure many times, which *[160]*Austin perceived long since, *tempestate contentionis, serenitas charitatis obnubilatur*, with this tempest of contention, the serenity of charity is overclouded, and there be too many spirits conjured up already in this kind in all sciences, and more than we can tell how to lay, which do so furiously rage, and keep such a racket, that as *[161]*Fabius said, It had been much better for some of them to have been born dumb, and altogether illiterate, than so far to dote to their own destruction.

At melius fuerat non scribere, namque tacere

Tutum semper erit,———*[162]*

'Tis a general fault, so Severinus the Dane complains *[163]*in physic, unhappy men as we are, we spend our days in unprofitable questions and disputations, intricate subtleties, *de lana caprina*about moonshine in the water, leaving in the mean time those chiefest treasures of nature untouched, wherein the best medicines for all manner of diseases are to be found, and do not only neglect them ourselves, but hinder, condemn, forbid, and scoff at others, that are willing to inquire after them. These motives at this present have induced me to make choice of this medicinal subject.

If any physician in the mean time shall infer, *Ne sutor ultra crepidam*, and find himself grieved that I have intruded into his profession, I will tell him in brief, I do not otherwise by them, than they do by us. If it be for their advantage, I know many of their sect which have taken orders, in hope of a benefice, 'tis a common transition, and why may not a melancholy divine, that can get nothing but by simony, profess physic? Drusianus an Italian (Crusianus, but corruptly, Trithemius calls him) *[164]*because he was not fortunate in his practice, forsook his profession, and writ afterwards in divinity. Marcilius Ficinus was *semel et simul*; a priest and a physician at once, and *[165]*T. Linacer in his old

age took orders. The Jesuits profess both at this time, divers of
them *permissu superiorum*, chirurgeons, panders, bawds, and midwives,
&c. Many poor country-vicars, for want of other means, are driven to
their shifts; to turn mountebanks, quacksalvers, empirics, and if our
greedy patrons hold us to such hard conditions, as commonly they do,
they will make most of us work at some trade, as Paul did, at last turn
taskers, maltsters, costermongers, graziers, sell ale as some have done,
or worse. Howsoever in undertaking this task, I hope I shall commit no
great error or *indecorum*, if all be considered aright, I can vindicate
myself with Georgius Braunus, and Hieronymus Hemingius, those two
learned divines; who (to borrow a line or two of mine *[166]*elder brother)
drawn by a natural love, the one of pictures and maps, prospectives and
chorographical delights, writ that ample theatre of cities; the other to the
study of genealogies, penned *theatrum genealogicum.* Or else I can excuse
my studies with *[167]*Lessius the Jesuit in like case. It is a disease of the
soul on which I am to treat, and as much appertaining to a divine as to a
physician, and who knows not what an agreement there is betwixt these
two professions? A good divine either is or ought to be a good physician,
a spiritual physician at least, as our Saviour calls himself, and was
indeed, Mat. iv. 23; Luke, v. 18; Luke, vii. 8. They differ but in object, the
one of the body, the other of the soul, and use divers medicines to cure;
one amends *animam per corpus*, the other *corpus per animam* as *[168]*our
Regius Professor of physic well informed us in a learned lecture of his not
long since. One helps the vices and passions of the soul, anger, lust,
desperation, pride, presumption, &c. by applying that spiritual physic; as
the other uses proper remedies in bodily diseases. Now this being a
common infirmity of body and soul, and such a one that hath as much
need of spiritual as a corporal cure, I could not find a fitter task to busy
myself about, a more apposite theme, so necessary, so commodious, and
generally concerning all sorts of men, that should so equally participate
of both, and require a whole physician. A divine in this compound mixed
malady can do little alone, a physician in some kinds of melancholy
much less, both make an absolute cure.
*[169]*Alterius sic altera poscit opem.

————when in friendship joined

A mutual succour in each other find.

And 'tis proper to them both, and I hope not unbeseeming me, who am
by my profession a divine, and by mine inclination a physician. I had
Jupiter in my sixth house; I say with *[170]*Beroaldus, *non sum medicus,
nec medicinae prorsus expers*, in the theory of physic I have taken some
pains, not with an intent to practice, but to satisfy myself, which was a
cause likewise of the first undertaking of this subject.

If these reasons do not satisfy thee, good reader, as Alexander Munificus
that bountiful prelate, sometimes bishop of Lincoln, when he had built
six castles, *ad invidiam operis eluendam*, saith *[171]*Mr. Camden, to take

xl

away the envy of his work (which very words Nubrigensis hath of Roger the rich bishop of Salisbury, who in king Stephen's time built Shirburn castle, and that of Devises), to divert the scandal or imputation, which might be thence inferred, built so many religious houses. If this my discourse be over-medicinal, or savour too much of humanity, I promise thee that I will hereafter make thee amends in some treatise of divinity. But this I hope shall suffice, when you have more fully considered of the matter of this my subject, *rem substratam*, melancholy, madness, and of the reasons following, which were my chief motives: the generality of the disease, the necessity of the cure, and the commodity or common good that will arise to all men by the knowledge of it, as shall at large appear in the ensuing preface. And I doubt not but that in the end you will say with me, that to anatomise this humour aright, through all the members of this our Microcosmus, is as great a task, as to reconcile those chronological errors in the Assyrian monarchy, find out the quadrature of a circle, the creeks and sounds of the north-east, or north-west passages, and all out as good a discovery as that hungry *[172]*Spaniard's of Terra Australis Incognita, as great trouble as to perfect the motion of Mars and Mercury, which so crucifies our astronomers, or to rectify the Gregorian Calendar. I am so affected for my part, and hope as *[173]*Theophrastus did by his characters, That our posterity, O friend Policles, shall be the better for this which we have written, by correcting and rectifying what is amiss in themselves by our examples, and applying our precepts and cautions to their own use. And as that great captain Zisca would have a drum made of his skin when he was dead, because he thought the very noise of it would put his enemies to flight, I doubt not but that these following lines, when they shall be recited, or hereafter read, will drive away melancholy (though I be gone) as much as Zisca's drum could terrify his foes. Yet one caution let me give by the way to my present, or my future reader, who is actually melancholy, that he read not the *[174]*symptoms or prognostics in this following tract, lest by applying that which he reads to himself, aggravating, appropriating things generally spoken, to his own person (as melancholy men for the most part do) he trouble or hurt himself, and get in conclusion more harm than good. I advise them therefore warily to peruse that tract, *Lapides loquitur* (so said *[175]*Agrippa *de occ. Phil.*) *et caveant lectores ne cerebrum iis excutiat.* The rest I doubt not they may securely read, and to their benefit. But I am over-tedious, I proceed.

Of the necessity and generality of this which I have said, if any man doubt, I shall desire him to make a brief survey of the world, as *[176]* Cyprian adviseth Donat, supposing himself to be transported to the top of some high mountain, and thence to behold the tumults and chances of this wavering world, he cannot choose but either laugh at, or pity it. S. Hierom out of a strong imagination, being in the wilderness, conceived with himself, that he then saw them dancing in Rome; and if thou shalt either conceive, or climb to see, thou shalt soon perceive that all the world is mad, that it is melancholy, dotes; that it is (which Epichthonius Cosmopolites expressed not many years since in a map) made like a fool's head (with that motto, *Caput helleboro dignum*) a crazed head, *cavea stultorum*, a fool's paradise, or as Apollonius, a common prison of gulls, cheaters, flatterers, &c. and needs to be reformed. Strabo in the ninth book of his geography, compares Greece to the picture of a man, which comparison of his, Nic. Gerbelius in his exposition of Sophianus' map, approves; the breast lies open from those Acroceraunian hills in Epirus, to the Sunian promontory in Attica; Pagae and Magaera are the two shoulders; that Isthmus of Corinth the neck; and Peloponnesus the head. If this allusion hold, 'tis sure a mad head; Morea may be Moria; and to speak what I think, the inhabitants of modern Greece swerve as much from reason and true religion at this day, as that Morea doth from the picture of a man. Examine the rest in like sort, and you shall find that kingdoms and provinces are melancholy, cities and families, all creatures, vegetal, sensible, and rational, that all sorts, sects, ages, conditions, are out of tune, as in Cebes' table, *omnes errorem bibunt*, before they come into the world, they are intoxicated by error's cup, from the highest to the lowest have need of physic, and those particular actions in *[177]*Seneca, where father and son prove one another mad, may be general; Porcius Latro shall plead against us all. For indeed who is not a fool, melancholy, mad?—*[178] Qui nil molitur inepte*, who is not brain-sick? Folly, melancholy, madness, are but one disease, *Delirium* is a common name to all. Alexander, Gordonius, Jason Pratensis, Savanarola, Guianerius, Montaltus, confound them as differing *secundum magis et minus*; so doth David, Psal. xxxvii. 5. I said unto the fools, deal not so madly, and 'twas an old Stoical paradox, *omnes stultos insanire, [179]*all fools are mad, though some madder than others. And who is not a fool, who is free from melancholy? Who is not touched more or less in habit or disposition? If in disposition, ill dispositions beget habits, if they persevere, saith *[180]*Plutarch, habits either are, or turn to diseases. 'Tis the same which Tully maintains in the second of his Tusculans, *omnium insipientum animi in morbo sunt, et perturbatorum*, fools are sick, and all that are troubled in mind: for what is sickness, but as *[181]*Gregory Tholosanus defines it, A dissolution or perturbation of the bodily league, which health combines: and who is not sick, or ill-disposed? in whom doth not passion, anger, envy, discontent, fear and sorrow reign? Who labours not of this disease? Give me but a little leave, and you shall see by what testimonies, confessions, arguments, I will evince it, that most men are mad, that they had as much need to go a pilgrimage to the Anticyrae (as in *[182]*Strabo's time they did) as in our days they run to Compostella, our Lady of Sichem, or Lauretta, to seek for help; that it is like to be as prosperous a voyage as that of Guiana, and that there is much more need of hellebore than of tobacco.

That men are so misaffected, melancholy, mad, giddy-headed, hear the testimony of Solomon, Eccl. ii. 12. And I turned to behold wisdom, madness and folly, &c. And ver. 23: All his days are sorrow, his travel grief, and his heart taketh no rest in the night. So that take melancholy in what sense you will, properly or improperly, in disposition or habit, for pleasure or for pain, dotage, discontent, fear, sorrow, madness, for part, or all, truly, or metaphorically, 'tis all one. Laughter itself is madness according to Solomon, and as St. Paul hath it, Worldly sorrow brings death. The hearts of the sons of men are evil, and madness is in their

hearts while they live, Eccl. ix. 3. Wise men themselves are no better. Eccl. i. 18. In the multitude of wisdom is much grief, and he that increaseth wisdom, increaseth sorrow, chap. ii. 17. He hated life itself, nothing pleased him: he hated his labour, all, as *[183]*he concludes, is sorrow, grief, vanity, vexation of spirit. And though he were the wisest man in the world, *sanctuarium sapientiae*, and had wisdom in abundance, he will not vindicate himself, or justify his own actions. Surely I am more foolish than any man, and have not the understanding of a man in me, Prov. xxx. 2. Be they Solomon's words, or the words of Agur, the son of Jakeh, they are canonical. David, a man after God's own heart, confesseth as much of himself, Psal. xxxvii. 21, 22. So foolish was I and ignorant, I was even as a beast before thee. And condemns all for fools, Psal. xciii.; xxxii. 9; xlix. 20. He compares them to beasts, horses, and mules, in which there is no understanding. The apostle Paul accuseth himself in like sort, 2 Cor. ix. 21. I would you would suffer a little my foolishness, I speak foolishly. The whole head is sick, saith Esay, and the heart is heavy, cap. i. 5. And makes lighter of them than of oxen and asses, the ox knows his owner, &c.: read Deut. xxxii. 6; Jer. iv.; Amos, iii. 1; Ephes. v. 6. Be not mad, be not deceived, foolish Galatians, who hath bewitched you? How often are they branded with this epithet of madness and folly? No word so frequent amongst the fathers of the Church and divines; you may see what an opinion they had of the world, and how they valued men's actions.
I know that we think far otherwise, and hold them most part wise men that are in authority, princes, magistrates, *[184]*rich men, they are wise men born, all politicians and statesmen must needs be so, for who dare speak against them? And on the other, so corrupt is our judgment, we esteem wise and honest men fools. Which Democritus well signified in an epistle of his to Hippocrates: *[185]*the Abderites account virtue madness, and so do most men living. Shall I tell you the reason of it? *[186]*Fortune and Virtue, Wisdom and Folly, their seconds, upon a time contended in the Olympics; every man thought that Fortune and Folly would have the worst, and pitied their cases; but it fell out otherwise. Fortune was blind and cared not where she stroke, nor whom, without laws, *Audabatarum instar*, &c. Folly, rash and inconsiderate, esteemed as little what she said or did. Virtue and Wisdom gave *[187]*place, were hissed out, and exploded by the common people; Folly and Fortune admired, and so are all their followers ever since: knaves and fools commonly fare and deserve best in worldlings' eyes and opinions. Many good men have no better fate in their ages: Achish, 1 Sam. xxi. 14, held David for a madman. *[188]*Elisha and the rest were no otherwise esteemed. David was derided of the common people, Ps. ix. 7, I am become a monster to many. And generally we are accounted fools for Christ, 1 Cor. xiv. We fools thought his life madness, and his end without honour, Wisd. v. 4. Christ and his Apostles were censured in like sort, John x.; Mark iii.; Acts xxvi. And so were all Christians in *[189]*Pliny's time, *fuerunt et alii, similis dementiae*, &c. And called not long after, *[190]*Vesaniae sectatores, eversores hominum, polluti novatores, fanatici, canes, malefici, venefici, Galilaei homunciones*, &c. 'Tis an ordinary thing with us, to account honest, devout, orthodox, divine,

religious, plain-dealing men, idiots, asses, that cannot, or will not lie and
dissemble, shift, flatter, *accommodare se ad eum locum ubi nati sunt,*
make good bargains, supplant, thrive, *patronis inservire; solennes
ascendendi modos apprehendere, leges, mores, consuetudines recte
observare, candide laudare, fortiter defendere, sententias amplecti,
dubitare de nullus, credere omnia, accipere omnia, nihil reprehendere,
caeteraque quae promotionem ferunt et securitatem, quae sine ambage
felicem, reddunt hominem, et vere sapientem apud nos*; that cannot
temporise as other men do, *[191]*hand and take bribes, &c. but fear God,
and make a conscience of their doings. But the Holy Ghost that knows
better how to judge, he calls them fools. The fool hath said in his
heart, Psal. liii. 1. And their ways utter their folly, Psal. xlix. 14. *[192]*For
what can be more mad, than for a little worldly pleasure to procure unto
themselves eternal punishment? As Gregory and others inculcate unto
us.
Yea even all those great philosophers the world hath ever had in
admiration, whose works we do so much esteem, that gave precepts of
wisdom to others, inventors of Arts and Sciences, Socrates the wisest
man of his time by the Oracle of Apollo, whom his two
scholars, *[193]*Plato and *[194]* Xenophon, so much extol and magnify
with those honourable titles, best and wisest of all mortal men, the
happiest, and most just; and as *[195]* Alcibiades incomparably
commends him; Achilles was a worthy man, but Bracides and others
were as worthy as himself; Antenor and Nestor were as good as Pericles,
and so of the rest; but none present, before, or after Socrates, *nemo
veterum neque eorum qui nunc sunt*, were ever such, will match, or come
near him. Those seven wise men of Greece, those Britain Druids, Indian
Brachmanni, Ethiopian Gymnosophist, Magi of the Persians, Apollonius,
of whom Philostratus, *Non doctus, sed natus sapiens*, wise from his
cradle, Eoicuras so much admired by his scholar Lucretius:
Qui genus humanum ingenio superavit, et omnes

Perstrinxit stellas exortus ut aetherius sol.

Whose wit excell'd the wits of men as far,

As the sun rising doth obscure a star,

Or that so much renowned Empedocles,
*[196]*Ut vix humana videatur stirpe creatus.

All those of whom we read such *[197]*hyperbolical eulogiums, as of
Aristotle, that he was wisdom itself in the abstract, *[198]*a miracle of
nature, breathing libraries, as Eunapius of Longinus, lights of nature,
giants for wit, quintessence of wit, divine spirits, eagles in the clouds,
fallen from heaven, gods, spirits, lamps of the world, dictators, *Nulla
ferant talem saecla futura virum*: monarchs, miracles, superintendents of
wit and learning, *oceanus, phoenix, atlas, monstrum, portentum hominis,
orbis universi musaeum, ultimus humana naturae donatus, naturae
maritus,*

———merito cui doctior orbis

Submissis defert fascibus imperium.

As Aelian writ of Protagoras and Gorgias, we may say of them all, *tantum a sapientibus abfuerunt, quantum a viris pueri*, they were children in respect, infants, not eagles, but kites; novices, illiterate, *Eunuchi sapientiae*. And although they were the wisest, and most admired in their age, as he censured Alexander, I do them, there were 10,000 in his army as worthy captains (had they been in place of command) as valiant as himself; there were myriads of men wiser in those days, and yet all short of what they ought to be. *[199]*Lactantius, in his book of wisdom, proves them to be dizzards, fools, asses, madmen, so full of absurd and ridiculous tenets, and brain-sick positions, that to his thinking never any old woman or sick person doted worse. *[200]*Democritus took all from Leucippus, and left, saith he, the inheritance of his folly to Epicurus, *[201]insanienti dum sapientiae*, &c. The like he holds of Plato, Aristippus, and the rest, making no difference *[202]*betwixt them and beasts, saving that they could speak. *[203]*Theodoret in his tract, *De cur. grec. affect.* manifestly evinces as much of Socrates, whom though that Oracle of Apollo confirmed to be the wisest man then living, and saved him from plague, whom 2000 years have admired, of whom some will as soon speak evil as of Christ, yet *re vera*, he was an illiterate idiot, as *[204]*Aristophanes calls him, *irriscor et ambitiosus*, as his master Aristotle terms him, *scurra Atticus*, as Zeno, an *[205]*enemy to all arts and sciences, as Athaeneus, to philosophers and travellers, an opiniative ass, a caviller, a kind of pedant; for his manners, as Theod. Cyrensis describes him, a *[206]* sodomite, an atheist, (so convict by Anytus) *iracundus et ebrius, dicax*, &c. a pot-companion, by *[207]*Plato's own confession, a sturdy drinker; and that of all others he was most sottish, a very madman in his actions and opinions. Pythagoras was part philosopher, part magician, or part witch. If you desire to hear more of Apollonius, a great wise man, sometime paralleled by Julian the apostate to Christ, I refer you to that learned tract of Eusebius against Hierocles, and for them all to Lucian's *Piscator, Icaromenippus, Necyomantia*: their actions, opinions in general were so prodigious, absurd, ridiculous, which they broached and maintained, their books and elaborate treatises were full of dotage, which Tully *ad Atticum* long since observed, *delirant plerumque scriptores in libris suis*, their lives being opposite to their words, they commended poverty to others, and were most covetous themselves, extolled love and peace, and yet persecuted one another with virulent hate and malice. They could give precepts for verse and prose, but not a man of them (as *[208]*Seneca tells them home) could moderate his affections. Their music did show us *flebiles modos*, &c. how to rise and fall, but they could not so contain themselves as in adversity not to make a lamentable tone. They will measure ground by geometry, set down limits, divide and subdivide, but cannot yet prescribe *quantum homini satis*, or keep within compass of reason and discretion. They can square circles, but understand not the state of their own souls, describe right lines and crooked, &c. but know not what is right in this life, *quid in vita rectum sit, ignorant*; so that as he said, *Nescio an Anticyram ratio illis destinet omnem*. I think all the Anticyrae will not restore them to their wits, *[209]*if these men now, that held *[210]*Xenodotus' heart, Crates' liver, Epictetus' lantern, were so sottish, and had no more brains than so many beetles, what shall we think of the commonalty? what of the rest?

Yea, but you will infer, that is true of heathens, if they be conferred with Christians, 1 Cor. iii. 19. The wisdom of this world is foolishness with God, earthly and devilish, as James calls it, iii. 15. They were vain in their imaginations, and their foolish heart was full of darkness, Rom. i. 21, 22. When they professed themselves wise, became fools. Their witty works are admired here on earth, whilst their souls are tormented in hell fire. In some sense, *Christiani Crassiani*, Christians are Crassians, and if compared to that wisdom, no better than fools. *Quis est sapiens? Solus Deus, [211]*Pythagoras replies, God is only wise, Rom. xvi. Paul determines only good, as Austin well contends, and no man living can be justified in his sight. God looked down from heaven upon the children of men, to see if any did understand, Psalm liii. 2, 3, but all are corrupt, err. Rom. iii. 12, None doeth good, no, not one. Job aggravates this, iv. 18, Behold he found no steadfastness in his servants, and laid folly upon his angels; 19. How much more on them that dwell in houses of clay? In this sense we are all fools, and the *[212]*Scripture alone is *arx Minervae*, we and our writings are shallow and imperfect. But I do not so mean; even in our ordinary dealings we are no better than fools. All our actions, as *[213]*Pliny told Trajan, upbraid us of folly, our whole course of life is but matter of laughter: we are not soberly wise; and the world itself, which ought at least to be wise by reason of his antiquity, as *[214]*Hugo de Prato Florido will have it, *semper stultizat*, is every day more foolish than other; the more it is whipped, the worse it is, and as a child will still be crowned with roses and flowers. We are apish in it, *asini bipedes*, and every place is full *inversorum Apuleiorum* of metamorphosed and two-legged asses, *inversorum Silenorum*, childish, *pueri instar bimuli, tremula patris dormientis in ulna*. Jovianus Pontanus, Antonio Dial, brings in some laughing at an old man, that by reason of his age was a little fond, but as he admonisheth there, *Ne mireris mi hospes de hoc sene*, marvel not at him only, for *tota haec civitas delirium*, all our town dotes in like sort, *[215]*we are a company of fools. Ask not with him in the poet, *[216]*Larvae hunc intemperiae insaniaeque agitant senem? What madness ghosts this old man, but what madness ghosts us all? For we are *ad unum omnes*, all mad, *semel insanivimus omnes* not once, but alway so, *et semel, et simul, et semper*, ever and altogether as bad as he; and not *senex bis puer, delira anus*, but say it of us all, *semper pueri*,

young and old, all dote, as Lactantius proves out of Seneca; and no difference betwixt us and children, saving that, *majora ludimus, et grandioribus pupis*, they play with babies of clouts and such toys, we sport with greater baubles. We cannot accuse or condemn one another, being faulty ourselves, *deliramenta loqueris*, you talk idly, or as [217]Mitio upbraided Demea, *insanis, auferte*, for we are as mad our own selves, and it is hard to say which is the worst. Nay, 'tis universally so, [218]*Vitam regit fortuna, non sapientia*.
When [219]Socrates had taken great pains to find out a wise man, and to that purpose had consulted with philosophers, poets, artificers, he concludes all men were fools; and though it procured him both anger and much envy, yet in all companies he would openly profess it.
When [220] Supputius in Pontanus had travelled all over Europe to confer with a wise man, he returned at last without his errand, and could find none. [221] Cardan concurs with him, Few there are (for aught I can perceive) well in their wits. So doth [222]Tully, I see everything to be done foolishly and unadvisedly.
Ille sinistrorsum, hic dextrorsum, unus utrique

Error, sed variis illudit partibus omnes.

One reels to this, another to that wall,

'Tis the same error that deludes them all.

[223]They dote all, but not alike, Μανία γαρ πᾶσιν ὁμοια, not in the same kind, One is covetous, a second lascivious, a third ambitious, a fourth envious, &c. as Damasippus the Stoic hath well illustrated in the poet,

[224]Desipiunt omnes aeque ac tu.

And they who call you fool, with equal claim

May plead an ample title to the name.

'Tis an inbred malady in every one of us, there is *seminarium stultitiae*, a seminary of folly, which if it be stirred up, or get ahead, will run *in infinitum*, and infinitely varies, as we ourselves are severally addicted, saith [225]Balthazar Castilio: and cannot so easily be rooted out, it takes such fast hold, as Tully holds, *altae radices stultitiae*, [226]so we are bred, and so we continue. Some say there be two main defects of wit, error and ignorance, to which all others are reduced; by ignorance we know not things necessary, by error we know them falsely. Ignorance is a privation, error a positive act. From ignorance comes vice, from error heresy, &c. But make how many kinds you will, divide and subdivide, few men are free, or that do not impinge on some one kind or other. [227]*Sic plerumque agitat stultos inscitia*, as he that examines his own and other men's actions shall find.

*[228]*Charon in Lucian, as he wittily feigns, was conducted by Mercury to such a place, where he might see all the world at once; after he had sufficiently viewed, and looked about, Mercury would needs know of him what he had observed: He told him that he saw a vast multitude and a promiscuous, their habitations like molehills, the men as emmets, he could discern cities like so many hives of bees, wherein every bee had a sting, and they did nought else but sting one another, some domineering like hornets bigger than the rest, some like filching wasps, others as drones.Over their heads were hovering a confused company of perturbations, hope, fear, anger, avarice, ignorance, &c., and a multitude of diseases hanging, which they still pulled on their pates. Some were brawling, some fighting, riding, running, *sollicite ambientes, callide litigantes* for toys and trifles, and such momentary things, Their towns and provinces mere factions, rich against poor, poor against rich, nobles against artificers, they against nobles, and so the rest. In conclusion, he condemned them all for madmen, fools, idiots, asses, *O stulti, quaenam haec est amentia?* O fools, O madmen, he exclaims, *insana studia, insani labores,* &c. Mad endeavours, mad actions, mad, mad, mad, *[229]O saeclum insipiens et infacetum,* a giddy-headed age. Heraclitus the philosopher, out of a serious meditation of men's lives, fell a weeping, and with continual tears bewailed their misery, madness, and folly. Democritus on the other side, burst out a laughing, their whole life seemed to him so ridiculous, and he was so far carried with this ironical passion, that the citizens of Abdera took him to be mad, and sent therefore ambassadors to Hippocrates, the physician, that he would exercise his skill upon him. But the story is set down at large by Hippocrates, in his epistle to Damogetus, which because it is not impertinent to this discourse, I will insert verbatim almost as it is delivered by Hippocrates himself, with all the circumstances belonging unto it.

When Hippocrates was now come to Abdera, the people of the city came flocking about him, some weeping, some intreating of him, that he would do his best. After some little repast, he went to see Democritus, the people following him, whom he found (as before) in his garden in the suburbs all alone, *[230]*sitting upon a stone under a plane tree, without hose or shoes, with a book on his knees, cutting up several beasts, and busy at his study. The multitude stood gazing round about to see the congress. Hippocrates, after a little pause, saluted him by his name, whom he resaluted, ashamed almost that he could not call him likewise by his, or that he had forgot it. Hippocrates demanded of him what he was doing: he told him that he was *[231]*busy in cutting up several beasts, to find out the cause of madness and melancholy. Hippocrates commended his work, admiring his happiness and leisure. And why, quoth Democritus, have not you that leisure? Because, replied Hippocrates, domestic affairs hinder, necessary to be done for ourselves, neighbours, friends; expenses, diseases, frailties and mortalities which happen; wife, children, servants, and such business which deprive us of our time. At this speech Democritus profusely laughed (his friends and the people standing by, weeping in the mean time, and lamenting his madness). Hippocrates asked the reason why he laughed. He told him, at the vanities and the fopperies of the time, to see men so empty of all virtuous actions, to hunt so far after gold, having no end of ambition; to take such infinite pains for a little glory, and to be favoured of men; to make such deep mines into the earth for gold, and many times to find nothing, with loss of their lives and fortunes. Some to love dogs, others horses, some to desire to be obeyed in many provinces,[232] and yet themselves will know no obedience. [233]Some to love their wives dearly at first, and after a while to forsake and hate them; begetting children, with much care and cost for their education, yet when they grow to man's estate, [234]to despise, neglect, and leave them naked to the world's mercy. [235]Do not these behaviours express their intolerable folly? When men live in peace, they covet war, detesting quietness, [236] deposing kings, and advancing others in their stead, murdering some men to beget children of their wives. How many strange humours are in men! When they are poor and needy, they seek riches, and when they have them, they do not enjoy them, but hide them under ground, or else wastefully spend them. O wise Hippocrates, I laugh at such things being done, but much more when no good comes of them, and when they are done to so ill purpose. There is no truth or justice found amongst them, for they daily plead one against another, [237]the son against the father and the mother, brother against brother, kindred and friends of the same quality; and all this for riches, whereof after death they cannot be possessors. And yet notwithstanding they will defame and kill one another, commit all unlawful actions, contemning God and men, friends and country. They make great account of many senseless things, esteeming them as a great part of their treasure, statues, pictures, and such like movables, dear bought, and so cunningly wrought, as nothing but speech wanteth in them, [238]and yet they hate living persons speaking to them. [239]Others affect difficult things; if they dwell on firm land they will remove to an island, and thence to land again, being no way constant to their desires. They commend courage and strength in wars, and let themselves be conquered by lust and avarice; they are, in brief, as disordered in their minds, as Thersites was in his body. And now, methinks, O most worthy Hippocrates, you should not reprehend my laughing, perceiving so many fooleries in men; [240]for no man will mock his own folly, but that which he seeth in a second, and so they justly mock one another. The drunkard calls him a glutton whom he knows to be sober. Many men love the sea, others husbandry; briefly, they cannot agree in their own trades and professions, much less in their lives and actions.

When Hippocrates heard these words so readily uttered, without premeditation, to declare the world's vanity, full of ridiculous contrariety, he made answer, that necessity compelled men to many such actions, and divers wills ensuing from divine permission, that we might not be idle, being nothing is so odious to them as sloth and negligence. Besides, men cannot foresee future events, in this uncertainty of human affairs; they would not so marry, if they could foretell the causes of their dislike and separation; or parents, if they knew the hour of their children's death, so tenderly provide for them; or an husbandman sow, if he thought there would be no increase; or a merchant adventure to sea, if he foresaw shipwreck; or be a magistrate, if presently to be deposed. Alas, worthy Democritus, every man hopes the best, and to that end he doth it, and therefore no such cause, or ridiculous occasion of laughter. Democritus hearing this poor excuse, laughed again aloud, perceiving he wholly mistook him, and did not well understand what he had said concerning perturbations and tranquillity of the mind. Insomuch, that if men would govern their actions by discretion and providence, they would not declare themselves fools as now they do, and he should have no cause of laughter; but (quoth he) they swell in this life as if they were immortal, and demigods, for want of understanding. It were enough to make them wise, if they would but consider the mutability of this world, and how it wheels about, nothing being firm and sure. He that is now above, tomorrow is beneath; he that sate on this side today, tomorrow is hurled on the other: and not considering these matters, they fall into many inconveniences and troubles, coveting things of no profit, and thirsting after them, tumbling headlong into many calamities. So that if men would attempt no more than what they can bear, they should lead contented lives, and learning to know themselves, would limit their ambition, *[241]*they would perceive then that nature hath enough without seeking such superfluities, and unprofitable things, which bring nothing with them but grief and molestation. As a fat body is more subject to diseases, so are rich men to absurdities and fooleries, to many casualties and cross inconveniences. There are many that take no heed what happeneth to others by bad conversation, and therefore overthrow themselves in the same manner through their own fault, not foreseeing dangers manifest. These are things (O more than mad, quoth he) that give me matter of laughter, by suffering the pains of your impieties, as your avarice, envy, malice, enormous villainies, mutinies, unsatiable desires, conspiracies, and other incurable vices; besides your *[242]*dissimulation and hypocrisy, bearing deadly hatred one to the other, and yet shadowing it with a good face, flying out into all filthy lusts, and transgressions of all laws, both of nature and civility. Many things which they have left off, after a while they fall to again, husbandry, navigation; and leave again, fickle and inconstant as they are. When they are young, they would be old, and old, young. *[243]* Princes commend a private life; private men itch after honour: a magistrate commends a quiet life; a quiet man would be in his office, and obeyed as he is: and what is the cause of all this, but that they know not themselves? Some delight to destroy, *[244]*one to build, another to spoil one country to enrich another and himself. *[245]*In all these things they are like children, in whom is no judgment or counsel and resemble beasts, saving that beasts are better than they, as being contented with nature. *[246]* When shall you see a lion hide gold in the ground, or a bull contend for better pasture? When a boar is thirsty, he drinks what will serve him, and no more; and when his belly is full, ceaseth to eat: but men are immoderate in both, as in lust—they covet carnal copulation at set times; men always, ruinating thereby the health of their bodies. And doth it not deserve laughter to see an amorous fool torment himself for a wench; weep, howl for a misshapen slut, a dowdy sometimes, that might have his choice of the finest beauties? Is there any remedy for this in physic? I do anatomise and cut up these poor beasts, *[247]*to see these distempers, vanities, and follies, yet such proof were better made on man's body, if my kind nature would endure it: *[248]*who from the hour of his birth is most miserable; weak, and sickly; when he sucks he is guided by others, when he is grown great practiseth unhappiness *[249]*and is sturdy, and when old, a child again, and repenteth him of his life past. And here being interrupted by one that brought books, he fell to it again, that all were mad, careless, stupid. To prove my former speeches, look into courts, or private houses. *[250]*Judges give judgment according to their own advantage, doing manifest wrong to poor innocents to please others. Notaries alter sentences, and for money lose their deeds. Some make false monies; others counterfeit false weights. Some abuse their parents, yea corrupt their own sisters; others make long libels and pasquils, defaming men of good life, and extol such as are lewd and vicious. Some rob one, some another: *[251]*magistrates make laws against thieves, and are the veriest thieves themselves. Some kill themselves, others despair, not obtaining their desires. Some dance, sing, laugh, feast and banquet, whilst others sigh, languish, mourn and lament, having neither meat, drink, nor clothes. *[252]*Some prank up their bodies, and have their minds full of execrable vices. Some trot about *[253]*to bear false witness, and say anything for money; and though judges know of it, yet for a bribe they wink at it, and suffer false contracts to prevail against equity. Women are all day a dressing, to pleasure other men abroad, and go like sluts at home, not caring to please their own husbands whom they should. Seeing men are so fickle, so sottish, so intemperate, why should not I laugh at those to whom *[254]*folly seems wisdom, will not be cured, and perceive it not?

It grew late: Hippocrates left him; and no sooner was he come away, but all the citizens came about flocking, to know how he liked him. He told them in brief, that notwithstanding those small neglects of his attire, body, diet, *[255]*the world had not a wiser, a more learned, a more honest man, and they were much deceived to say that he was mad.

Thus Democritus esteemed of the world in his time, and this was the cause of his laughter: and good cause he had.

*[256]*Olim jure quidem, nunc plus Democrite ride;

Quin rides? vita haec nunc mage ridicula est.

Democritus did well to laugh of old,

Good cause he had, but now much more;

This life of ours is more ridiculous

Than that of his, or long before.

Never so much cause of laughter as now, never so many fools and madmen. 'Tis not one *[257]*Democritus will serve turn to laugh in these days; we have now need of a Democritus to laugh at Democritus; one jester to flout at another, one fool to fleer at another: a great stentorian Democritus, as big as that Rhodian Colossus, For now, as *[258]*Salisburiensis said in his time, *totus mundus histrionem agit,* the whole world plays the fool; we have a new theatre, a new scene, a new comedy of errors, a new company of personate actors, *volupiae sacra* (as Calcagninus willingly feigns in his Apologues) are celebrated all the world over, *[259]*where all the actors were madmen and fools, and every hour changed habits, or took that which came next. He that was a mariner today, is an apothecary tomorrow; a smith one while, a philosopher another, *in his volupiae ludis*; a king now with his crown, robes, sceptre, attendants, by and by drove a loaded ass before him like a carter, &c. If Democritus were alive now, he should see strange alterations, a new company of counterfeit vizards, whifflers, Cumane asses, maskers, mummers, painted puppets, outsides, fantastic shadows, gulls, monsters, giddy-heads, butterflies. And so many of them are indeed (*[260]*if all be true that I have read). For when Jupiter and Juno's wedding was solemnised of old, the gods were all invited to the feast, and many noble men besides: Amongst the rest came Crysalus, a Persian prince, bravely attended, rich in golden attires, in gay robes, with a majestical presence, but otherwise an ass. The gods seeing him come in such pomp and state, rose up to give him place, *ex habitu hominem metientes*; *[261]*but Jupiter perceiving what he was, a light, fantastic, idle fellow, turned him and his proud followers into butterflies: and so they continue still (for aught I know to the contrary) roving about in pied coats, and are called chrysalides by the wiser sort of men: that is, golden outsides, drones, and flies, and things of no worth. Multitudes of such, &c.

[262]————ubique invenies

Stultos avaros, sycopliantas prodigos.

Many additions, much increase of madness, folly, vanity, should Democritus observe, were he now to travel, or could get leave of Pluto to come see fashions, as Charon did in Lucian to visit our cities of Moronia Pia, and Moronia Felix: sure I think he would break the rim of his belly with laughing. *[263]Si foret in terris rideret Democritus, seu,* &c.

A satirical Roman in his time, thought all vice, folly, and madness were all at full sea, *[264]Omne in praecipiti vitium stetit.*
*[265]*Josephus the historian taxeth his countrymen Jews for bragging of their vices, publishing their follies, and that they did contend amongst themselves who should be most notorious in villainies; but we flow higher in madness, far beyond them, *[266]*Mox daturi progeniem vitiosorem,

And yet with crimes to us unknown,

Our sons shall mark the coming age their own,

and the latter end (you know whose oracle it is) is like to be worse. 'Tis not to be denied, the world alters every day, *Ruunt urbes, regna transferuntur, &c. variantur habitus, leges innovantur,* as *[267]*Petrarch observes, we change language, habits, laws, customs, manners, but not vices, not diseases, not the symptoms of folly and madness, they are still the same. And as a river, we see, keeps the like name and place, but not water, and yet ever runs, *[268]Labitur et labetur in omne volubilis aevum*; our times and persons alter, vices are the same, and ever will be; look how nightingales sang of old, cocks crowed, kine lowed, sheep bleated, sparrows chirped, dogs barked, so they do still: we keep our madness still, play the fools still, *nec dum finitus Orestes*; we are of the same humours and inclinations as our predecessors were; you shall find us all alike, much at one, we and our sons, *Et nati natorum, et qui nascuntur ab illis.* And so shall our posterity continue to the last. But to speak of times present.

If Democritus were alive now, and should but see the superstition of our age, our *[269]*religious madness, as *[270]*Meteran calls it, *Religiosam insaniam,* so many professed Christians, yet so few imitators of Christ; so much talk of religion, so much science, so little conscience; so much knowledge, so many preachers, so little practice; such variety of sects, such have and hold of all sides, *[271]—obvia signis Signa,* &c., such absurd and ridiculous traditions and ceremonies: If he should meet a *[272]* Capuchin, a Franciscan, a Pharisaical Jesuit, a man-serpent, a shave-crowned Monk in his robes, a begging Friar, or, see their three-crowned Sovereign Lord the Pope, poor Peter's successor, *servus servorum Dei,* to depose kings with his foot, to tread on emperors' necks, make them stand barefoot and barelegged at his gates, hold his bridle and stirrup, &c. (O that Peter and Paul were alive to see this!) If he should observe a *[273]*prince creep so devoutly to kiss his toe, and those red-cap cardinals, poor parish priests of old, now princes' companions; what would he say? *Coelum ipsum petitur stultitia.* Had he met some of our devout pilgrims going barefoot to Jerusalem, our lady of Lauretto, Rome, S. Iago, S. Thomas' Shrine, to creep to those counterfeit and maggot-eaten relics; had he been present at a mass, and seen such kissing of paxes, crucifixes, cringes, duckings, their several attires and ceremonies, pictures of saints, *[274]*indulgences, pardons, vigils, fasting, feasts, crossing, knocking, kneeling at Ave-Marias, bells, with many such; —*jucunda rudi spectacula plebi,[275]* praying in gibberish, and mumbling of beads. Had he heard an old woman say her prayers in Latin, their sprinkling of holy water, and going a procession, *[276]*————incedunt monachorum agmina mille;

Quid momerem vexilla, cruces, idolaque culta, &c.

Their breviaries, bulls, hallowed beans, exorcisms, pictures, curious crosses, fables, and baubles. Had he read the Golden Legend, the Turks' Alcoran, or Jews' Talmud, the Rabbins' Comments, what would he have thought? How dost thou think he might have been affected? Had he more particularly examined a Jesuit's life amongst the rest, he should have seen an hypocrite profess poverty, *[277]*and yet possess more goods and lands than many princes, to have infinite treasures and revenues; teach others to fast, and play the gluttons themselves; like watermen that row one way and look another. *[278]*Vow virginity, talk of holiness, and yet indeed a notorious bawd, and famous fornicator, *lascivum pecus*, a very goat. Monks by profession, *[279]*such as give over the world, and the vanities of it, and yet a Machiavellian rout *[280]*interested in all manner of state: holy men, peace-makers, and yet composed of envy, lust, ambition, hatred, and malice; firebrands, *adulta patriae pestis*, traitors, assassinats, *hac itur ad astra*, and this is to supererogate, and merit heaven for themselves and others. Had he seen on the adverse side, some of our nice and curious schismatics in another extreme, abhor all ceremonies, and rather lose their lives and livings, than do or admit anything Papists have formerly used, though in things indifferent (they alone are the true Church, *sal terrae, cum sint omnium insulsissimi*). Formalists, out of fear and base flattery, like so many weather-cocks turn round, a rout of temporisers, ready to embrace and maintain all that is or shall be proposed in hope of preferment: another Epicurean company, lying at lurch as so many vultures, watching for a prey of Church goods, and ready to rise by the downfall of any: as *[281]*Lucian said in like case, what dost thou think Democritus would have done, had he been spectator of these things?

Or had he but observed the common people follow like so many sheep one of their fellows drawn by the horns over a gap, some for zeal, some for fear, *quo se cunque rapit tempestas*, to credit all, examine nothing, and yet ready to die before they will adjure any of those ceremonies to which they have been accustomed; others out of hypocrisy frequent sermons, knock their breasts, turn up their eyes, pretend zeal, desire reformation, and yet professed usurers, gripers, monsters of men, harpies, devils in their lives, to express nothing less.

What would he have said to see, hear, and read so many bloody battles, so many thousands slain at once, such streams of blood able to turn mills: *unius ob noxam furiasque*, or to make sport for princes, without any just cause, *[282]*for vain titles (saith Austin), precedency, some wench, or such like toy, or out of desire of domineering, vainglory, malice, revenge, folly, madness,(goodly causes all, *ob quas universus orbis bellis et caedibus misceatur*,) whilst statesmen themselves in the mean time are secure at home, pampered with all delights and pleasures, take their ease, and follow their lusts, not considering what intolerable misery poor soldiers endure, their often wounds, hunger, thirst, &c., the lamentable cares, torments, calamities, and oppressions that accompany such proceedings, they feel not, take no notice of it. So wars are begun, by the persuasion of a few debauched, hair-brain, poor, dissolute, hungry captains, parasitical fawners, unquiet hotspurs, restless innovators, green heads, to satisfy one man's private spleen, lust, ambition, avarice, &c.; *tales rapiunt scelerata in praelia causae. Flos hominum*, proper men, well proportioned, carefully brought up, able both in body and mind, sound, led like so many *[283]*beasts to the slaughter in the flower of their years, pride, and full strength, without all remorse and pity, sacrificed to Pluto, killed up as so many sheep, for devils' food, 40,000 at once. At once, said I, that were tolerable, but these wars last always, and for many ages; nothing so familiar as this hacking and hewing, massacres, murders, desolations—*ignoto coelum clangore remugit*, they care not what mischief they procure, so that they may enrich themselves for the present; they will so long blow the coals of contention, till all the world be consumed with fire. The *[284]*siege of Troy lasted ten years, eight months, there died 870,000 Grecians, 670,000 Trojans, at the taking of the city, and after were slain 276,000 men, women, and children of all sorts. Caesar killed a million, *[285]*Mahomet the second Turk, 300,000 persons; Sicinius Dentatus fought in a hundred battles, eight times in single combat he overcame, had forty wounds before, was rewarded with 140 crowns, triumphed nine times for his good service. M. Sergius had 32 wounds; Scaeva, the Centurion, I know not how many; every nation had their Hectors, Scipios, Caesars, and Alexanders! Our *[286]*Edward the Fourth was in 26 battles afoot: and as they do all, he glories in it, 'tis related to his honour. At the siege of Hierusalem, 1,100,000 died with sword and famine. At the battle of Cannas, 70,000 men were slain, as *[287]*Polybius records, and as many at Battle Abbey with us; and 'tis no news to fight from sun to sun, as they did, as Constantine and Licinius, &c. At the siege of Ostend (the devil's academy) a poor town in respect, a small fort, but a great grave, 120,000 men lost their lives, besides whole towns, dorps, and hospitals, full of maimed soldiers; there were engines, fireworks, and whatsoever the devil could invent to do mischief with 2,500,000 iron bullets shot of 40 pounds weight, three or four millions of gold consumed. *[288]*Who (saith mine author) can be sufficiently amazed at their flinty hearts, obstinacy, fury, blindness, who without any likelihood of good success, hazard poor soldiers, and lead them without pity to the slaughter, which may justly be called the rage of furious beasts, that run without reason upon their own deaths:*[289]quis malus genius, quae furia quae pestis*, &c.; what plague, what fury brought so devilish, so brutish a thing as war first into men's minds? Who made so soft and peaceable a creature, born to love, mercy, meekness, so to rave, rage like beasts, and run on to their own destruction? how may Nature expostulate with mankind, *Ego te divinum animal finxi*, &c.? I made thee an harmless, quiet, a divine creature: how may God expostulate, and all good men? yet, *horum facta* (as *[290]*one condoles) *tantum admirantur, et heroum numero habent*: these are the brave spirits, the gallants of the world, these admired alone, triumph alone, have statues, crowns, pyramids, obelisks to their eternal fame, that immortal genius attends on them, *hac itur ad astra*. When Rhodes was besieged, *[291]fossae urbis cadaveribus repletae sunt*, the ditches were full of dead carcases: and as when the said Suleiman, great Turk, beleaguered Vienna, they lay level with the top of the walls. This they make a sport of, and will do it to their friends and confederates, against oaths, vows, promises, by treachery or otherwise; *[292]—dolus an virtus? quis in hoste requirat?* leagues and laws of arms, (*[293]silent leges inter arma*,) for their advantage, *omnia jura, divina, humana, proculcata plerumque sunt*; God's and men's laws are trampled under foot, the sword alone determines all; to satisfy their lust and spleen, they care not what they attempt, say, or do, *[294]Rara fides, probitasque viris qui castra sequuntur.* Nothing so common as to have *[295]* father fight against the son, brother against brother, kinsman against kinsman, kingdom against kingdom, province against province, Christians against Christians: *a quibus nec unquam cogitatione fuerunt laesi,* of whom they never had offence in thought, word, or deed. Infinite treasures consumed, towns burned, flourishing cities sacked and ruinated, *quodque animus meminisse horret,* goodly countries depopulated and left desolate, old inhabitants expelled, trade and traffic decayed, maids deflowered, *Virgines nondum thalamis jugatae, et comis nondum positis ephaebi;* chaste matrons cry out with Andromache, *[296]Concubitum mox cogar pati ejus, qui interemit Hectorem,* they shall be compelled peradventure to lie with them that erst killed their husbands: to see rich, poor, sick, sound, lords, servants, *eodem omnes incommodo macti,* consumed all or maimed, &c. *Et quicquid gaudens scelere animus audet, et perversa mens,* saith Cyprian, and whatsoever torment, misery, mischief, hell itself, the devil, *[297]* fury and rage can invent to their own ruin and destruction; so abominable a thing is *[298]*war, as Gerbelius concludes, *adeo foeda et abominanda res est bellum, ex quo hominum caedes, vastationes,* &c., the scourge of God, cause, effect, fruit and punishment of sin, and not *tonsura humani generis* as Tertullian calls it, but *ruina.* Had Democritus been present at the late civil wars in France, those abominable wars—*bellaque matribus detestata, [299]*where in less than ten years, ten thousand men were consumed, saith Collignius, twenty thousand churches overthrown; nay, the whole kingdom subverted (as *[300]*Richard Dinoth adds). So many myriads of the commons were butchered up, with sword, famine, war, *tanto odio utrinque ut barbari ad abhorrendam lanienam obstupescerent,* with such feral hatred, the world was amazed at it: or at our late Pharsalian fields in the time of Henry the Sixth, betwixt the houses of Lancaster and York, a hundred thousand men slain, *[301]*one writes; *[302]*another, ten thousand families were rooted out, that no man can but marvel, saith Comineus, at that barbarous immanity, feral madness, committed betwixt men of the same nation, language, and religion. *[303]Quis furor, O cives?* Why do the Gentiles so furiously rage, saith the Prophet David, Psal. ii. 1. But we may ask, why do the Christians so furiously rage? *[304]Arma volunt, quare poscunt, rapiuntque juventus?* Unfit for Gentiles, much less for us so to tyrannise, as the Spaniard in the West Indies, that killed up in 42 years (if we may believe *[305]*Bartholomeus a Casa, their own bishop) 12 millions of men, with stupend and exquisite torments; neither should I lie (said he) if I said 50 millions. I omit those French massacres, Sicilian evensongs, *[306]*the Duke of Alva's tyrannies, our gunpowder machinations, and that fourth fury, as *[307]*one calls it, the Spanish inquisition, which quite obscures those ten persecutions, *[308]——— saevit toto Mars impius orbe.* Is not this *[309]mundus furiosus,* a mad world, as he terms it, *insanum bellum?* are not these mad men, as *[310]*Scaliger concludes, *qui in praelio acerba morte, insaniae, suae memoriam pro perpetuo teste relinquunt posteritati;* which leave so

frequent battles, as perpetual memorials of their madness to all
succeeding ages? Would this, think you, have enforced our Democritus
to laughter, or rather made him turn his tune, alter his tone, and weep
with *[311]*Heraclitus, or rather howl, *[312]*roar, and tear his hair in
commiseration, stand amazed; or as the poets feign, that Niobe was for
grief quite stupefied, and turned to a stone? I have not yet said the worst,
that which is more absurd and *[313]*mad, in their tumults, seditions, civil
and unjust wars, *[314]*quod stulte sucipitur, impie geritur, misere finitur.
Such wars I mean; for all are not to be condemned, as those fantastical
Anabaptists vainly conceive. Our Christian tactics are all out as
necessary as the Roman acies, or Grecian phalanx, to be a soldier is a
most noble and honourable profession (as the world is), not to be spared,
they are our best walls and bulwarks, and I do therefore acknowledge
that of *[315]*Tully to be most true, All our civil affairs, all our studies, all
our pleading, industry, and commendation lies under the protection of
warlike virtues, and whensoever there is any suspicion of tumult, all our
arts cease; wars are most behoveful, *et bellatores agricolis civitati sunt
utiliores*, as *[316]*Tyrius defends: and valour is much to be commended in
a wise man; but they mistake most part, *auferre, trucidare, rapere, falsis
nominibus virtutem vocant*, &c. ('Twas Galgacus' observation in Tacitus)
they term theft, murder, and rapine, virtue, by a wrong name, rapes,
slaughters, massacres, &c. *jocus et ludus*, are pretty pastimes, as
Ludovicus Vives notes. *[317]*They commonly call the most hair-brain
bloodsuckers, strongest thieves, the most desperate villains, treacherous
rogues, inhuman murderers, rash, cruel and dissolute caitiffs,
courageous and generous spirits, heroical and worthy
captains, *[318]*brave men at arms, valiant and renowned soldiers,
possessed with a brute persuasion of false honour, as Pontus Huter in
his Burgundian history complains. By means of which it comes to pass
that daily so many voluntaries offer themselves, leaving their sweet
wives, children, friends, for sixpence (if they can get it) a day, prostitute
their lives and limbs, desire to enter upon breaches, lie sentinel, perdu,
give the first onset, stand in the fore front of the battle, marching bravely
on, with a cheerful noise of drums and trumpets, such vigour and
alacrity, so many banners streaming in the air, glittering armours,
motions of plumes, woods of pikes, and swords, variety of colours, cost
and magnificence, as if they went in triumph, now victors to the Capitol,
and with such pomp, as when Darius' army marched to meet Alexander
at Issus. Void of all fear they run into imminent dangers, cannon's
mouth, &c., *ut vulneribus suis ferrum hostium hebetent*,
saith *[319]*Barletius, to get a name of valour, humour and applause,
which lasts not either, for it is but a mere flash this fame, and like a
rose, *intra diem unum extinguitur*, 'tis gone in an instant. Of 15,000
proletaries slain in a battle, scarce fifteen are recorded in history, or one
alone, the General perhaps, and after a while his and their names are
likewise blotted out, the whole battle itself is forgotten. Those Grecian
orators, *summa vi ingenii et eloquentiae*, set out the renowned overthrows
at Thermopylae, Salamis, Marathon, Micale, Mantinea, Cheronaea,
Plataea. The Romans record their battle at Cannas, and Pharsalian
fields, but they do but record, and we scarce hear of them. And yet this

supposed honour, popular applause, desire of immortality by this means, pride and vainglory spur them on many times rashly and unadvisedly, to make away themselves and multitudes of others. Alexander was sorry, because there were no more worlds for him to conquer, he is admired by some for it, *animosa vox videtur, et regia*, 'twas spoken like a Prince; but as wise *[320]*Seneca censures him, 'twas *vox inquissima et stultissima*, 'twas spoken like a Bedlam fool; and that sentence which the same *[321]*Seneca appropriates to his father Philip and him, I apply to them all, *Non minores fuere pestes mortalium quam inundatio, quam conflagratio, quibus*, &c. they did as much mischief to mortal men as fire and water, those merciless elements when they rage. *[322]*Which is yet more to be lamented, they persuade them this hellish course of life is holy, they promise heaven to such as venture their lives *bello sacro*, and that by these bloody wars, as Persians, Greeks, and Romans of old, as modern Turks do now their commons, to encourage them to fight, *ut cadant infeliciter.* If they die in the field, they go directly to heaven, and shall be canonised for saints. (O diabolical invention!) put in the Chronicles, *in perpetuam rei memoriam*, to their eternal memory: when as in truth, as *[323]*some hold, it were much better (since wars are the scourge of God for sin, by which he punisheth mortal men's peevishness and folly) such brutish stories were suppressed, because *ad morum institutionem nihil habent*, they conduce not at all to manners, or good life. But they will have it thus nevertheless, and so they put note of *[324]*divinity upon the most cruel and pernicious plague of human kind, adore such men with grand titles, degrees, statues, images, *[325]*honour, applaud, and highly reward them for their good service, no greater glory than to die in the field. So Africanus is extolled by Ennius: Mars, and *[326]*Hercules, and I know not how many besides of old, were deified; went this way to heaven, that were indeed bloody butchers, wicked destroyers, and troublers of the world, prodigious monsters, hell-hounds, feral plagues, devourers, common executioners of human kind, as Lactantius truly proves, and Cyprian to Donat, such as were desperate in wars, and precipitately made away themselves, (like those Celts in Damascen, with ridiculous valour, *ut dedecorosum putarent muro ruenti se subducere*, a disgrace to run away for a rotten wall, now ready to fall on their heads,) such as will not rush on a sword's point, or seek to shun a cannon's shot, are base cowards, and no valiant men. By which means, *Madet orbis mutuo sanguine*, the earth wallows in her own blood,
*[327]*Savit amor ferri et scelerati insania belli; and for that, which if it be done in private, a man shall be rigorously executed, *[328]*and which is no less than murder itself; if the same fact be done in public in wars, it is called manhood, and the party is honoured for it.
[329]———Prosperum et felix scelus,

Virtus vocatur.———

We measure all as Turks do, by the event, and most part, as Cyprian notes, in all ages, countries, places, *saevitiae magnitudo impunitatem sceleris acquirit*; the foulness of the fact vindicates the offender. *[330]*One is crowned for that which another is tormented: *Ille crucem sceleris precium tulit, hic diadema*; made a knight, a lord, an earl, a great duke, (as *[331]*Agrippa notes) for that which another should have hung in gibbets, as a terror to the rest,

[332]——et tamen alter,

Si fecisset idem, caderet sub judice morum.

A poor sheep-stealer is hanged for stealing of victuals, compelled peradventure by necessity of that intolerable cold, hunger, and thirst, to save himself from starving: but a *[333]*great man in office may securely rob whole provinces, undo thousands, pill and poll, oppress *ad libitum*, flea, grind, tyrannise, enrich himself by spoils of the commons, be uncontrollable in his actions, and after all, be recompensed with turgent titles, honoured for his good service, and no man dare find fault, or *[334]* mutter at it.

How would our Democritus have been affected to see a wicked caitiff or *[335]*fool, a very idiot, a funge, a golden ass, a monster of men, to have many good men, wise, men, learned men to attend upon him with all submission, as an appendix to his riches, for that respect alone, because he hath more wealth and money, *[336]*to honour him with divine titles, and bombast epithets,to smother him with fumes and eulogies, whom they know to be a dizzard, a fool, a covetous wretch, a beast, &c. because he is rich? To see *sub exuviis leonis onagrum*, a filthy loathsome carcass, a Gorgon's head puffed up by parasites, assume this unto himself, glorious titles, in worth an infant, a Cuman ass, a painted sepulchre, an Egyptian temple? To see a withered face, a diseased, deformed, cankered complexion, a rotten carcass, a viperous mind, and Epicurean soul set out with orient pearls, jewels, diadems, perfumes, curious elaborate works, as proud of his clothes as a child of his new coats; and a goodly person, of an angel-like divine countenance, a saint, an humble mind, a meet spirit clothed in rags, beg, and now ready to be starved? To see a silly contemptible sloven in apparel, ragged in his coat, polite in speech, of a divine spirit, wise? another neat in clothes, spruce, full of courtesy, empty of grace, wit, talk nonsense?
To see so many lawyers, advocates, so many tribunals, so little justice; so many magistrates, so little care of common good; so many laws, yet never more disorders; *Tribunal litium segetem*, the Tribunal a labyrinth, so many thousand suits in one court sometimes, so violently followed? To see *injustissimum saepe juri praesidentem, impium religioni, imperitissimum eruditioni, otiosissimum labori, monstrosum humanitati?* to see a lamb *[337]*executed, a wolf pronounce sentence, *latro* arraigned, and *fur* sit on the bench, the judge severely punish others, and do worse himself, *[338] cundem furtum facere et punire, [339]rapinam plectere, quum sit ipse raptor?* Laws altered, misconstrued, interpreted pro and con, as the *[340]*judge is made by friends, bribed, or otherwise affected as a nose of wax, good today, none tomorrow; or firm in his opinion, cast in

his? Sentence prolonged, changed, *ad arbitrium judicis*, still the same case, *[341]*one thrust out of his inheritance, another falsely put in by favour, false forged deeds or wills. *Incisae leges negliguntur*, laws are made and not kept; or if put in execution, *[342]*they be some silly ones that are punished. As, put case it be fornication, the father will disinherit or abdicate his child, quite cashier him (out, villain, be gone, come no more in my sight); a poor man is miserably tormented with loss of his estate perhaps, goods, fortunes, good name, for ever disgraced, forsaken, and must do penance to the utmost; a mortal sin, and yet make the worst of it, *nunquid aliud fecit*, saith Tranio in the *[343]*poet, *nisi quod faciunt summis nati generibus?* he hath done no more than what gentlemen usually do. *[344]Neque novum, neque mirum, neque secus quam alii solent.* For in a great person, right worshipful Sir, a right honourable grandee, 'tis not a venial sin, no, not a peccadillo, 'tis no offence at all, a common and ordinary thing, no man takes notice of it; he justifies it in public, and peradventure brags of it,
*[345]*Nam quod turpe bonis, Titio, Seioque, decebat

Crispinum———

For what would be base in good men, Titius, and Seius, became Crispinus.

*[346]*Many poor men, younger brothers, &c. by reason of bad policy and idle education (for they are likely brought up in no calling), are compelled to beg or steal, and then hanged for theft; than which, what can be more ignominious, *non minus enim turpe principi multa supplicia, quam medico multa funera*, 'tis the governor's fault. *Libentius verberant quam docent*, as schoolmasters do rather correct their pupils, than teach them when they do amiss. *[347]*They had more need provide there should be no more thieves and beggars, as they ought with good policy, and take away the occasions, than let them run on, as they do to their own destruction: root out likewise those causes of wrangling, a multitude of lawyers, and compose controversies, *lites lustrales et seculares*, by some more compendious means. Whereas now for every toy and trifle they go to law, *[348]Mugit litibus insanum forum, et saevit invicem discordantium rabies*, they are ready to pull out one another's throats; and for commodity *[349]*to squeeze blood, saith Hierom, out of their brother's heart, defame, lie, disgrace, backbite, rail, bear false witness, swear, forswear, fight and wrangle, spend their goods, lives, fortunes, friends, undo one another, to enrich an harpy advocate, that preys upon them both, and cries *Eia Socrates, Eia Xantippe*; or some corrupt judge, that like the *[350]*kite in Aesop, while the mouse and frog fought, carried both away. Generally they prey one upon another as so many ravenous birds, brute beasts, devouring fishes, no medium, *[351]omnes hic aut captantur aut captant; aut cadavera quae lacerantur, aut corvi qui lacerant*, either deceive or be deceived; tear others or be torn in pieces themselves; like so

many buckets in a well, as one riseth another falleth, one's empty, another's full; his ruin is a ladder to the third; such are our ordinary proceedings. What's the market? A place, according to *[352]*Anacharsis, wherein they cozen one another, a trap; nay, what's the world itself? *[353]*A vast chaos, a confusion of manners, as fickle as the air, *domicilium insanorum*, a turbulent troop full of impurities, a mart of walking spirits, goblins, the theatre of hypocrisy, a shop of knavery, flattery, a nursery of villainy, the scene of babbling, the school of giddiness, the academy of vice; a warfare, *ubi velis nolis pugnandum, aut vincas aut succumbas*, in which kill or be killed; wherein every man is for himself, his private ends, and stands upon his own guard. No charity, *[354]*love, friendship, fear of God, alliance, affinity, consanguinity, Christianity, can contain them, but if they be any ways offended, or that string of commodity be touched, they fall foul. Old friends become bitter enemies on a sudden for toys and small offences, and they that erst were willing to do all mutual offices of love and kindness, now revile and persecute one another to death, with more than Vatinian hatred, and will not be reconciled. So long as they are behoveful, they love, or may bestead each other, but when there is no more good to be expected, as they do by an old dog, hang him up or cashier him: which *[355]* Cato counts a great indecorum, to use men like old shoes or broken glasses, which are flung to the dunghill; he could not find in his heart to sell an old ox, much less to turn away an old servant: but they instead of recompense, revile him, and when they have made him an instrument of their villainy, as *[356]*Bajazet the second Emperor of the Turks did by Acomethes Bassa, make him away, or instead of *[357]*reward, hate him to death, as Silius was served by Tiberius. In a word, every man for his own ends. Our *summum bonum* is commodity, and the goddess we adore *Dea moneta*, Queen money, to whom we daily offer sacrifice, which steers our hearts, hands, *[358]*affections, all: that most powerful goddess, by whom we are reared, depressed, elevated, *[359]*esteemed the sole commandress of our actions, for which we pray, run, ride, go, come, labour, and contend as fishes do for a crumb that falleth into the water. It's not worth, virtue, (that's *bonum theatrale,*) wisdom, valour, learning, honesty, religion, or any sufficiency for which we are respected, but *[360]*money, greatness, office, honour, authority; honesty is accounted folly; knavery, policy; *[361]*men admired out of opinion, not as they are, but as they seem to be: such shifting, lying, cogging, plotting, counterplotting, temporizing, nattering, cozening, dissembling, *[362]*that of necessity one must highly offend God if he be conformable to the world, *Cretizare cum Crete*, or else live in contempt, disgrace and misery. One takes upon him temperance, holiness, another austerity, a third an affected kind of simplicity, when as indeed, he, and he, and he, and the rest are *[363]*hypocrites, ambidexters, outsides, so many turning pictures, a lion on the one side, a lamb on the other. *[364]*How would Democritus have been affected to see these things!

To see a man turn himself into all shapes like a chameleon, or as Proteus, *omnia transformans sese in miracula rerum*, to act twenty parts and persons at once, for his advantage, to temporise and vary like Mercury the planet, good with good; bad with bad; having a several face, garb, and character for every one he meets; of all religions, humours, inclinations; to fawn like a spaniel, *mentitis et mimicis obsequis*; rage like a lion, bark like a cur, fight like a dragon, sting like a serpent, as meek as a lamb, and yet again grin like a tiger, weep like a crocodile, insult over some, and yet others domineer over him, here command, there crouch, tyrannise in one place, be baffled in another, a wise man at home, a fool abroad to make others merry.

To see so much difference betwixt words and deeds, so many parasangs betwixt tongue and heart, men like stage-players act variety of parts, *[365]*give good precepts to others, soar aloft, whilst they themselves grovel on the ground.

To see a man protest friendship, kiss his hand, *[366]*quem mallet truncatum videre, *[367]*smile with an intent to do mischief, or cozen him whom he salutes, *[368]*magnify his friend unworthy with hyperbolical eulogiums; his enemy albeit a good man, to vilify and disgrace him, yea all his actions, with the utmost that livor and malice can invent.

To see a *[369]*servant able to buy out his master, him that carries the mace more worth than the magistrate, which Plato, *lib. 11, de leg.*, absolutely forbids, Epictetus abhors. A horse that tills the *[370]*land fed with chaff, an idle jade have provender in abundance; him that makes shoes go barefoot himself, him that sells meat almost pined; a toiling drudge starve, a drone flourish.

To see men buy smoke for wares, castles built with fools' heads, men like apes follow the fashions in tires, gestures, actions: if the king laugh, all laugh;

*[371]*Rides? majore chachiano

Concutitur, flet si lachrymas conspexit amici.

*[372]*Alexander stooped, so did his courtiers; Alphonsus turned his head, and so did his parasites. *[373]*Sabina Poppea, Nero's wife, wore amber-coloured hair, so did all the Roman ladies in an instant, her fashion was theirs.

To see men wholly led by affection, admired and censured out of opinion without judgment: an inconsiderate multitude, like so many dogs in a village, if one bark all bark without a cause: as fortune's fan turns, if a man be in favour, or commanded by some great one, all the world applauds him; *[374]*if in disgrace, in an instant all hate him, and as at the sun when he is eclipsed, that erst took no notice, now gaze and stare upon him.

To see a man *[375]*wear his brains in his belly, his guts in his head, an hundred oaks on his back, to devour a hundred oxen at a meal, nay more, to devour houses and towns, or as those Anthropophagi, *[376]*to eat one another.

To see a man roll himself up like a snowball, from base beggary to right worshipful and right honourable titles, unjustly to screw himself into honours and offices; another to starve his genius, damn his soul to gather wealth, which he shall not enjoy, which his prodigal son melts and consumes in an instant. *[377]*

To see the κακοζηλίαν of our times, a man bend all his forces, means, time, fortunes, to be a favorite's favorite's favorite, &c., a parasite's parasite's parasite, that may scorn the servile world as having enough already.

To see an hirsute beggar's brat, that lately fed on scraps, crept and whined, crying to all, and for an old jerkin ran of errands, now ruffle in silk and satin, bravely mounted, jovial and polite, now scorn his old friends and familiars, neglect his kindred, insult over his betters, domineer over all.

To see a scholar crouch and creep to an illiterate peasant for a meal's meat; a scrivener better paid for an obligation; a falconer receive greater wages than a student; a lawyer get more in a day than a philosopher in a year, better reward for an hour, than a scholar for a twelvemonth's study; him that can *[378]*paint Thais, play on a fiddle, curl hair, &c., sooner get preferment than a philologer or a poet.

To see a fond mother, like Aesop's ape, hug her child to death, a *[379]* wittol wink at his wife's honesty, and too perspicuous in all other affairs; one stumble at a straw, and leap over a block; rob Peter, and pay Paul; scrape unjust sums with one hand, purchase great manors by corruption, fraud and cozenage, and liberally to distribute to the poor with the other, give a remnant to pious uses, &c. Penny wise, pound foolish; blind men judge of colours; wise men silent, fools talk; *[380]* find fault with others, and do worse themselves; *[381]*denounce that in public which he doth in secret; and which Aurelius Victor gives out of Augustus, severely censure that in a third, of which he is most guilty himself.

To see a poor fellow, or an hired servant venture his life for his new master that will scarce give him his wages at year's end; A country colon toil and moil, till and drudge for a prodigal idle drone, that devours all the gain, or lasciviously consumes with fantastical expenses; A noble man in a bravado to encounter death, and for a small flash of honour to cast away himself; A worldling tremble at an executor, and yet not fear hell-fire; To wish and hope for immortality, desire to be happy, and yet by all means avoid death, a necessary passage to bring him to it.

To see a foolhardy fellow like those old Danes, *qui decollari malunt quam verberari*, die rather than be punished, in a sottish humour embrace death with alacrity, yet *[382]*scorn to lament his own sins and miseries, or his clearest friends' departures.

To see wise men degraded, fools preferred, one govern towns and cities, and yet a silly woman overrules him at home; *[383]*Command a province, and yet his own servants or children prescribe laws to him, as

Themistocles' son did in Greece; *[384]*What I will (said he) my mother
will, and what my mother will, my father doth. To see horses ride in a
coach, men draw it; dogs devour their masters; towers build masons;
children rule; old men go to school; women wear the
breeches; *[385]*sheep demolish towns, devour men, &c. And in a word,
the world turned upside downward. *O viveret Democritus.*
*[386]*To insist in every particular were one of Hercules' labours, there's so
many ridiculous instances, as motes in the sun. *Quantum est in rebus
inane?* (How much vanity there is in things!) And who can speak of
all? *Crimine ab uno disce omnes*, take this for a taste.
But these are obvious to sense, trivial and well known, easy to be
discerned. How would Democritus have been moved, had he
seen *[387]*the secrets of their hearts? If every man had a window in his
breast, which Momus would have had in Vulcan's man, or that which
Tully so much wished it were written in every man's forehead, *Quid
quisque de republica sentiret*, what he thought; or that it could be effected
in an instant, which Mercury did by Charon in Lucian, by touching of his
eyes, to make him discern *semel et simul rumores et susurros.*
Spes hominum caecas, morbos, votumque labores,

Et passim toto volitantes aethere curas.

Blind hopes and wishes, their thoughts and affairs,

Whispers and rumours, and those flying cares.

That he could *cubiculorum obductas foras recludere et secreta cordium
penetrare*, which *[388]*Cyprian desired, open doors and locks, shoot bolts,
as Lucian's Gallus did with a feather of his tail: or Gyges' invisible ring,
or some rare perspective glass, or *Otacousticon*, which would so multiply
species, that a man might hear and see all at once (as *[389]* Martianus
Capella's Jupiter did in a spear which he held in his hand, which did
present unto him all that was daily done upon the face of the earth),
observe cuckolds' horns, forgeries of alchemists, the philosopher's stone,
new projectors, &c., and all those works of darkness, foolish vows,
hopes, fears and wishes, what a deal of laughter would it have afforded?
He should have seen windmills in one man's head, an hornet's nest in
another. Or had he been present with Icaromenippus in Lucian at
Jupiter's whispering place, *[390]*and heard one pray for rain, another for
fair weather; one for his wife's, another for his father's death, &c.; to ask
that at God's hand which they are abashed any man should hear: How
would he have been confounded? Would he, think you, or any man else,
say that these men were well in their wits? *Haec sani esse hominis quis
sanus juret Orestes?* Can all the hellebore in the Anticyrae cure these
men? No, sure, *[391]*an acre of hellebore will not do it.

That which is more to be lamented, they are mad like Seneca's blind
woman, and will not acknowledge, or *[392]*seek for any cure of it,
for *pauci vident morbum suum, omnes amant*. If our leg or arm offend us,
we covet by all means possible to redress it; *[393]*and if we labour of a
bodily disease, we send for a physician; but for the diseases of the mind
we take no notice of them: *[394]*Lust harrows us on the one side; envy,
anger, ambition on the other. We are torn in pieces by our passions, as
so many wild horses, one in disposition, another in habit; one is
melancholy, another mad; *[395]*and which of us all seeks for help, doth
acknowledge his error, or knows he is sick? As that stupid fellow put out
the candle because the biting fleas should not find him; he shrouds
himself in an unknown habit, borrowed titles, because nobody should
discern him. Every man thinks with himself, *Egomet videor mihi sanus*, I
am well, I am wise, and laughs at others. And 'tis a general fault amongst
them all, that *[396]* which our forefathers have approved, diet, apparel,
opinions, humours, customs, manners, we deride and reject in our time
as absurd. Old men account juniors all fools, when they are mere
dizzards; and as to sailors, ———*terraeque urbesque recedunt*——— they
move, the land stands still, the world hath much more wit, they dote
themselves. Turks deride us, we them; Italians Frenchmen, accounting
them light headed fellows, the French scoff again at Italians, and at their
several customs; Greeks have condemned all the world but themselves of
barbarism, the world as much vilifies them now; we account Germans
heavy, dull fellows, explode many of their fashions; they as contemptibly
think of us; Spaniards laugh at all, and all again at them. So are we fools
and ridiculous, absurd in our actions, carriages, diet, apparel, customs,
and consultations; we *[397]* scoff and point one at another, when as in
conclusion all are fools, *[398]* and they the veriest asses that hide their
ears most. A private man if he be resolved with himself, or set on an
opinion, accounts all idiots and asses that are not affected as he
is, *[399]*———*nil rectum, nisi quod placuit sibi, ducit*, that are not so
minded, *[400]*(*quodque volunt homines se bene velle putant*,) all fools that
think not as he doth: he will not say with Atticus, *Suam quisque
sponsam, mihi meam*, let every man enjoy his own spouse; but his alone
is fair, *suus amor*, &c. and scorns all in respect of himself *[401]*will
imitate none, hear none *[402]*but himself, as Pliny said, a law and
example to himself. And that which Hippocrates, in his epistle to
Dionysius, reprehended of old, is verified in our times, *Quisque in alio
superfluum esse censet, ipse quod non habet nec curat*, that which he
hath not himself or doth not esteem, he accounts superfluity, an idle
quality, a mere foppery in another: like Aesop's fox, when he had lost his
tail, would have all his fellow foxes cut off theirs. The Chinese say, that
we Europeans have one eye, they themselves two, all the world else is
blind: (though *[403]*Scaliger accounts them brutes too, *merum pecus*,) so
thou and thy sectaries are only wise, others indifferent, the rest beside
themselves, mere idiots and asses. Thus not acknowledging our own
errors and imperfections, we securely deride others, as if we alone were
free, and spectators of the rest, accounting it an excellent thing, as
indeed it is, *Aliena optimum frui insania*, to make ourselves merry with
other men's obliquities, when as he himself is more faulty than the

rest, *mutato nomine, de te fabula narratur*, he may take himself by the
nose for a fool; and which one calls *maximum stultitiae specimen*, to be
ridiculous to others, and not to perceive or take notice of it, as Marsyas
was when he contended with Apollo, *non intelligens se deridiculo haberi*,
saith *[404]* Apuleius; 'tis his own cause, he is a convicted madman,
as *[405]*Austin well infers in the eyes of wise men and angels he seems
like one, that to our thinking walks with his heels upwards. So thou
laughest at me, and I at thee, both at a third; and he returns that of the
poet upon us again, *[406]Hei mihi, insanire me aiunt, quum ipsi ultro
insaniant*. We accuse others of madness, of folly, and are the veriest
dizzards ourselves. For it is a great sign and property of a fool
(which Eccl. x. 3, points at) out of pride and self-conceit to insult, vilify,
condemn, censure, and call other men fools (*Non videmus manticae quod
a tergo est*) to tax that in others of which we are most faulty; teach that
which we follow not ourselves: For an inconstant man to write of
constancy, a profane liver prescribe rules of sanctity and piety, a dizzard
himself make a treatise of wisdom, or with Sallust to rail downright at
spoilers of countries, and yet in *[407]*office to be a most grievous poller
himself. This argues weakness, and is an evident sign of such parties'
indiscretion. *[408]Peccat uter nostrum cruce dignius?* Who is the fool
now? Or else peradventure in some places we are all mad for company,
and so 'tis not seen, *Satietas erroris et dementiae, pariter absurditatem et
admirationem tollit*. 'Tis with us, as it was of old (in *[409]*Tully's censure
at least) with C. Pimbria in Rome, a bold, hair-brain, mad fellow, and so
esteemed of all, such only excepted, that were as mad as himself: now in
such a case there is *[410]*no notice taken of it.
Nimirum insanus paucis videatur; eo quod

Maxima pars hominum morbo jactatur eodem.

When all are mad, where all are like opprest

Who can discern one mad man from the rest?

But put case they do perceive it, and some one be manifestly convicted of
madness, *[411]*he now takes notice of his folly, be it in action, gesture,
speech, a vain humour he hath in building, bragging, jangling, spending,
gaming, courting, scribbling, prating, for which he is ridiculous to
others, *[412]*on which he dotes, he doth acknowledge as much: yet with
all the rhetoric thou hast, thou canst not so recall him, but to the
contrary notwithstanding, he will persevere in his dotage. 'Tis *amabilis
insania, et mentis gratissimus error*, so pleasing, so delicious, that
he *[413]* cannot leave it. He knows his error, but will not seek to decline
it, tell him what the event will be, beggary, sorrow, sickness, disgrace,
shame, loss, madness, yet *[414]*an angry man will prefer vengeance, a
lascivious his whore, a thief his booty, a glutton his belly, before his
welfare. Tell an epicure, a covetous man, an ambitious man of his
irregular course, wean him from it a little, *pol me occidistis amici*, he cries

anon, you have undone him, and as *[415]*a dog to his vomit, he returns to it again; no persuasion will take place, no counsel, say what thou canst,

Clames licet et mare coelo

————Confundas, surdo narras,*[416]*

demonstrate as Ulysses did to *[417]*Elpenor and Gryllus, and the rest of his companions those swinish men, he is irrefragable in his humour, he will be a hog still; bray him in a mortar, he will be the same. If he be in an heresy, or some perverse opinion, settled as some of our ignorant Papists are, convince his understanding, show him the several follies and absurd fopperies of that sect, force him to say, *veris vincor*, make it as clear as the sun, *[418]*he will err still, peevish and obstinate as he is; and as he said *[419]*si *in hoc erro, libenter erro, nec hunc errorem auferri mihi volo*; I will do as I have done, as my predecessors have done, *[420]*and as my friends now do: I will dote for company. Say now, are these men *[421]*mad or no, *[422]*Heus age responde? are they ridiculous? *cedo quemvis arbitrum*, are they *sanae mentis*, sober, wise, and discreet? have they common sense? ————*[423]*uter est insanior horum? I am of Democritus' opinion for my part, I hold them worthy to be laughed at; a company of brain-sick dizzards, as mad as *[424]*Orestes and Athamas, that they may go ride the ass, and all sail along to the Anticyrae, in the ship of fools for company together. I need not much labour to prove this which I say otherwise than thus, make any solemn protestation, or swear, I think you will believe me without an oath; say at a word, are they fools? I refer it to you, though you be likewise fools and madmen yourselves, and I as mad to ask the question; for what said our comical Mercury?

*[425]*Justum ab injustis petere insipientia est.

I'll stand to your censure yet, what think you?

But forasmuch as I undertook at first, that kingdoms, provinces, families, were melancholy as well as private men, I will examine them in particular, and that which I have hitherto dilated at random, in more general terms, I will particularly insist in, prove with more special and evident arguments, testimonies, illustrations, and that in brief. *[426]*Nunc accipe quare desipiant omnes aeque ac tu. My first argument is borrowed from Solomon, an arrow drawn out of his sententious quiver, Pro. iii. 7, Be not wise in thine own eyes. And xxvi. 12, Seest thou a man wise in his own conceit? more hope is of a fool than of him. Isaiah pronounceth a woe against such men, cap. v. 21, that are wise in their own eyes, and prudent in their own sight. For hence we may gather, that it is a great offence, and men are much deceived that think too well of themselves, an especial argument to convince them of folly. Many men (saith *[427]*Seneca) had been without question wise, had they not had an opinion that they had attained to perfection of knowledge already, even before they had gone half way, too forward, too ripe, *praeproperi*, too quick and ready, *[428]cito prudentes, cito pii, cito mariti, cito patres, cito sacerdotes, cito omnis officii capaces et curiosi*, they had too good a conceit of themselves, and that marred all; of their worth, valour, skill, art, learning, judgment, eloquence, their good parts; all their geese are swans, and that manifestly proves them to be no better than fools. In former times they had but seven wise men, now you can scarce find so many fools. Thales sent the golden tripos, which the fishermen found, and the oracle commanded to be *[429]* given to the wisest, to Bias, Bias to Solon, &c. If such a thing were now found, we should all fight for it, as the three goddesses did for the golden apple, we are so wise: we have women politicians, children metaphysicians; every silly fellow can square a circle, make perpetual motions, find the philosopher's stone, interpret Apocalypses, make new Theories, a new system of the world, new Logic, new Philosophy, &c. *Nostra utique regio*, saith *[430]*Petronius, our country is so full of deified spirits, divine souls, that you may sooner find a God than a man amongst us, we think so well of ourselves, and that is an ample testimony of much folly.

My second argument is grounded upon the like place of Scripture, which though before mentioned in effect, yet for some reasons is to be repeated (and by Plato's good leave, I may do it, *[431]*δίς τὸ καλὸν ρηθέν οὐδέν βλάπτει) Fools (saith David) by reason of their transgressions. &c. Psal. cvii. 17. Hence Musculus infers all transgressors must needs be fools. So we read Rom. ii., Tribulation and anguish on the soul of every man that doeth evil; but all do evil. And Isaiah, lxv. 14, My servant shall sing for joy, and *[432]*ye shall cry for sorrow of heart, and vexation of mind. 'Tis ratified by the common consent of all philosophers. Dishonesty (saith Cardan) is nothing else but folly and madness. *[433] Probus quis nobiscum vivit?* Show me an honest man, *Nemo malus qui non stultus*, 'tis Fabius' aphorism to the same end. If none honest, none wise, then all fools. And well may they be so accounted: for who will account him otherwise, *Qui iter adornat in occidentem, quum properaret in orientem?* that goes backward all his life, westward, when he is bound to the east? or hold him a wise man (saith *[434]*Musculus) that prefers momentary pleasures to eternity, that spends his master's goods in his absence, forthwith to be condemned for it? *Nequicquam sapit qui sibi non sapit*, who will say that a sick man is wise, that eats and drinks to overthrow the temperature of his body? Can you account him wise or discreet that would willingly have his health, and yet will do nothing that should procure or continue it? *[435]*Theodoret, out of Plotinus the Platonist, holds it a ridiculous thing for a man to live after his own laws, to do that which is offensive to God, and yet to hope that he should save him: and when he voluntarily neglects his own safety, and contemns the means, to think to be delivered by another: who will say these men are wise?

A third argument may be derived from the precedent, *[436]*all men are carried away with passion, discontent, lust, pleasures, &c., they generally hate those virtues they should love, and love such vices they should hate. Therefore more than melancholy, quite mad, brute beasts, and void of reason, so Chrysostom contends; or rather dead and buried alive, as *[437]* Philo Judeus concludes it for a certainty, of all such that are carried away with passions, or labour of any disease of the mind. Where is fear and sorrow, there *[438]*Lactantius stiffly maintains, wisdom cannot dwell,

———qui cupiet, metuet quoque porro,

Qui metuens vivit, liber mihi non erit unquam.*[439]*

Seneca and the rest of the stoics are of opinion, that where is any the least perturbation, wisdom may not be found. What more ridiculous, as *[440]*Lactantius urges, than to hear how Xerxes whipped the Hellespont, threatened the Mountain Athos, and the like. To speak *ad rem*, who is free from passion? *[441]Mortalis nemo est quem non attingat dolor, morbusve*, as *[442]*Tully determines out of an old poem, no mortal men can avoid sorrow and sickness, and sorrow is an inseparable companion from melancholy. *[443]*Chrysostom pleads farther yet, that they are more than mad, very beasts, stupefied and void of common sense: For how (saith he) shall I know thee to be a man, when thou kickest like an ass, neighest like a horse after women, ravest in lust like a bull, ravenest like a bear, stingest like a scorpion, rakest like a wolf, as subtle as a fox, as impudent as a dog? Shall I say thou art a man, that hast all the symptoms of a beast? How shall I know thee to be a man? by thy shape? That affrights me more, when I see a beast in likeness of a man.

*[444]*Seneca calls that of Epicurus, *magnificam vocem*, an heroical speech, A fool still begins to live, and accounts it a filthy lightness in men, every day to lay new foundations of their life, but who doth otherwise? One travels, another builds; one for this, another for that business, and old folks are as far out as the rest; *O dementem senectutem*, Tully exclaims. Therefore young, old, middle age, are all stupid, and dote.
*[445]*Aeneas Sylvius, amongst many other, sets down three special ways to find a fool by. He is a fool that seeks that he cannot find: he is a fool that seeks that, which being found will do him more harm than good: he is a fool, that having variety of ways to bring him to his journey's end, takes that which is worst. If so, methinks most men are fools; examine their courses, and you shall soon perceive what dizzards and mad men the major part are.
Beroaldus will have drunkards, afternoon men, and such as more than ordinarily delight in drink, to be mad. The first pot quencheth thirst, so Panyasis the poet determines in *Athenaeus, secunda gratiis, horis et Dyonisio*: the second makes merry, the third for pleasure, *quarta, ad*

insaniam, the fourth makes them mad. If this position be true, what a catalogue of mad men shall we have? what shall they be that drink four times four? *Nonne supra omnem furorem, supra omnem insanian reddunt insanissimos?* I am of his opinion, they are more than mad, much worse than mad.

The *[446]*Abderites condemned Democritus for a mad man, because he was sometimes sad, and sometimes again profusely merry. *Hac Patria* (saith Hippocrates) *ob risum furere et insanire dicunt*, his countrymen hold him mad because he laughs; *[447]*and therefore he desires him to advise all his friends at Rhodes, that they do not laugh too much, or be over sad. Had those Abderites been conversant with us, and but seen what *[448]* fleering and grinning there is in this age, they would certainly have concluded, we had been all out of our wits.

Aristotle in his Ethics holds *felix idemque sapiens*, to be wise and happy, are reciprocal terms, *bonus idemque sapiens honestus.* 'Tis *[449]* Tully's paradox, wise men are free, but fools are slaves, liberty is a power to live according to his own laws, as we will ourselves: who hath this liberty? who is free?

[450]————sapiens sibique imperiosus,

Quem neque pauperis, neque mors, neque vincula terrent,

Responsare cupidinibus, contemnere honores

Fortis, et in seipso totus teres atque rotundus.

He is wise that can command his own will,

Valiant and constant to himself still,

Whom poverty nor death, nor bands can fright,

Checks his desires, scorns honours, just and right.

But where shall such a man be found? If no where, then *e diametro*, we are all slaves, senseless, or worse. *Nemo malus felix.* But no man is happy in this life, none good, therefore no man wise.*[451]Rari quippe boni*———— For one virtue you shall find ten vices in the same party; *pauci Promethei, multi Epimethei.* We may peradventure usurp the name, or attribute it to others for favour, as Carolus Sapiens, Philippus Bonus, Lodovicus Pius, &c., and describe the properties of a wise man, as Tully doth an orator, Xenophon Cyrus, Castilio a courtier, Galen temperament, an aristocracy is described by politicians. But where shall such a man be found?

Vir bonus et sapiens, qualem vix repperit unum

Millibus e multis hominum consultus Apollo.

A wise, a good man in a million,

Apollo consulted could scarce find one.

A man is a miracle of himself, but Trismegistus adds, *Maximum miraculum homo sapiens*, a wise man is a wonder: *multi Thirsigeri, pauci Bacchi*.
Alexander when he was presented with that rich and costly casket of king Darius, and every man advised him what to put in it, he reserved it to keep Homer's works, as the most precious jewel of human wit, and yet *[452]* Scaliger upbraids Homer's muse, *Nutricem insanae sapientiae*, a nursery of madness, *[453]*impudent as a court lady, that blushes at nothing. Jacobus Mycillus, Gilbertus Cognatus, Erasmus, and almost all posterity admire Lucian's luxuriant wit, yet Scaliger rejects him in his censure, and calls him the Cerberus of the muses. Socrates, whom all the world so much magnified, is by Lactantius and Theodoret condemned for a fool. Plutarch extols Seneca's wit beyond all the Greeks, *nulli secundus*, yet *[454]* Seneca saith of himself, when I would solace myself with a fool, I reflect upon myself, and there I have him. Cardan, in his Sixteenth Book of Subtleties, reckons up twelve supereminent, acute philosophers, for worth, subtlety, and wisdom: Archimedes, Galen, Vitruvius, Architas Tarentinus, Euclid, Geber, that first inventor of Algebra, Alkindus the Mathematician, both Arabians, with others. But his *triumviri terrarum* far beyond the rest, are Ptolomaeus, Plotinus, Hippocrates. Scaliger *exercitat. 224*, scoffs at this censure of his, calls some of them carpenters and mechanicians, he makes Galen *fimbriam Hippocratis*, a skirt of Hippocrates: and the said *[455]*Cardan himself elsewhere condemns both Galen and Hippocrates for tediousness, obscurity, confusion. Paracelsus will have them both mere idiots, infants in physic and philosophy. Scaliger and Cardan admire Suisset the Calculator, *qui pene modum excessit humani ingenii*, and yet *[456]*Lod. Vives calls them *nugas Suisseticas*: and Cardan, opposite to himself in another place, contemns those ancients in respect of times present, *[457]*Majoresque nostros ad presentes collatos juste pueros appellari*. In conclusion, the said *[458]*Cardan and Saint Bernard will admit none into this catalogue of wise men, *[459]*but only prophets and apostles; how they esteem themselves, you have heard before. We are worldly-wise, admire ourselves, and seek for applause: but hear Saint *[460]*Bernard, *quanto magis foras es sapiens, tanto magis intus stultus efficeris*, &c. *in omnibus es prudens, circa teipsum insipiens*: the more wise thou art to others, the more fool to thyself. I may not deny but that there is some folly approved, a divine fury, a holy madness, even a spiritual drunkenness in the saints of God themselves; *sanctum insanium* Bernard calls it (though not as blaspheming *[461]*Vorstius, would infer it as a passion incident to God himself, but) familiar to good men, as that of Paul, 2 Cor. he was a fool, &c. and Rom. ix. he wisheth himself to be anathematised for them. Such is that drunkenness which Ficinus speaks of, when the soul is elevated and ravished with a divine taste of that heavenly nectar, which poets deciphered by the sacrifice of Dionysius, and in this sense with the poet, *[462]insanire lubet*, as Austin

exhorts us, *ad ebrietatem se quisque paret*, let's all be mad
and *[463]*drunk. But we commonly mistake, and go beyond our
commission, we reel to the opposite part, *[464]*we are not capable of
it, *[465]*and as he said of the Greeks, *Vos Graeci semper pueri, vos
Britanni, Galli, Germani, Itali*, &c. you are a company of fools.
Proceed now *a partibus ad totum*, or from the whole to parts, and you
shall find no other issue, the parts shall be sufficiently dilated in this
following Preface. The whole must needs follow by a sorites or induction.
Every multitude is mad, *[466]*bellua *multorum capitum*, (a many-headed
beast), precipitate and rash without judgment, *stultum animal*, a roaring
rout. *[467]*Roger Bacon proves it out of Aristotle, *Vulgus dividi in
oppositum contra sapientes, quod vulgo videtur verum, falsum est*; that
which the commonalty accounts true, is most part false, they are still
opposite to wise men, but all the world is of this humour (*vulgus*), and
thou thyself art *de vulgo*, one of the commonalty; and he, and he, and so
are all the rest; and therefore, as Phocion concludes, to be approved in
nought you say or do, mere idiots and asses. Begin then where you will,
go backward or forward, choose out of the whole pack, wink and choose,
you shall find them all alike, never a barrel better herring.
Copernicus, Atlas his successor, is of opinion, the earth is a planet,
moves and shines to others, as the moon doth to us. Digges, Gilbert,
Keplerus, Origanus, and others, defend this hypothesis of his in sober
sadness, and that the moon is inhabited: if it be so that the earth is a
moon, then are we also giddy, vertiginous and lunatic within this
sublunary maze.
I could produce such arguments till dark night: if you should hear the
rest,
Ante diem clauso component vesper Olimpo:

Through such a train of words if I should run,

The day would sooner than the tale be done:

but according to my promise, I will descend to particulars. This
melancholy extends itself not to men only, but even to vegetals and
sensibles. I speak not of those creatures which are saturnine,
melancholy by nature, as lead, and such like minerals, or those plants,
rue, cypress, &c. and hellebore itself, of which *[468]*Agrippa treats,
fishes, birds, and beasts, hares, conies, dormice, &c., owls, bats,
nightbirds, but that artificial, which is perceived in them all. Remove a
plant, it will pine away, which is especially perceived in date trees, as you
may read at large in Constantine's husbandry, that antipathy betwixt the
vine and the cabbage, vine and oil. Put a bird in a cage, he will die for
sullenness, or a beast in a pen, or take his young ones or companions
from him, and see what effect it will cause. But who perceives not these
common passions of sensible creatures, fear, sorrow, &c. Of all other,
dogs are most subject to this malady, insomuch some hold they dream
as men do, and through violence of melancholy run mad; I could relate

many stories of dogs that have died for grief, and pined away for loss of their masters, but they are common in every *[469]*author.

Kingdoms, provinces, and politic bodies are likewise sensible and subject to this disease, as *[470]*Boterus in his politics hath proved at large. As in human bodies (saith he) there be divers alterations proceeding from humours, so be there many diseases in a commonwealth, which do as diversely happen from several distempers, as you may easily perceive by their particular symptoms. For where you shall see the people civil, obedient to God and princes, judicious, peaceable and quiet, rich, fortunate, *[471]*and flourish, to live in peace, in unity and concord, a country well tilled, many fair built and populous cities, *ubi incolae nitent* as old *[472]*Cato said, the people are neat, polite and terse, *ubi bene, beateque vivunt,* which our politicians make the chief end of a commonwealth; and which *[473]* Aristotle, *Polit. lib. 3, cap. 4,* calls *Commune bonum,* Polybius *lib. 6, optabilem et selectum statum,* that country is free from melancholy; as it was in Italy in the time of Augustus, now in China, now in many other flourishing kingdoms of Europe. But whereas you shall see many discontents, common grievances, complaints, poverty, barbarism, beggary, plagues, wars, rebellions, seditions, mutinies, contentions, idleness, riot, epicurism, the land lie untilled, waste, full of bogs, fens, deserts, &c., cities decayed, base and poor towns, villages depopulated, the people squalid, ugly, uncivil; that kingdom, that country, must needs be discontent, melancholy, hath a sick body, and had need to be reformed.
Now that cannot well be effected, till the causes of these maladies be first removed, which commonly proceed from their own default, or some accidental inconvenience: as to be situated in a bad clime, too far north, sterile, in a barren place, as the desert of Libya, deserts of Arabia, places void of waters, as those of Lop and Belgian in Asia, or in a bad air, as at Alexandretta, Bantam, Pisa, Durrazzo, S. John de Ulloa, &c., or in danger of the sea's continual inundations, as in many places of the Low Countries and elsewhere, or near some bad neighbours, as Hungarians to Turks, Podolians to Tartars, or almost any bordering countries, they live in fear still, and by reason of hostile incursions are oftentimes left desolate. So are cities by reason *[474]*of wars, fires, plagues, inundations, *[475]*wild beasts, decay of trades, barred havens, the sea's violence, as Antwerp may witness of late, Syracuse of old, Brundusium in Italy, Rye and Dover with us, and many that at this day suspect the sea's fury and rage, and labour against it as the Venetians to their inestimable charge. But the most frequent maladies are such as proceed from themselves, as first when religion and God's service is neglected, innovated or altered, where they do not fear God, obey their prince, where atheism, epicurism, sacrilege, simony, &c., and all such impieties are freely committed, that country cannot prosper. When Abraham came to Gerar, and saw a bad land, he said, sure the fear of God was not in that place. *[476]* Cyprian Echovius, a Spanish chorographer, above all other cities of Spain, commends Borcino, in which there was no beggar, no man poor, &c., but all rich, and in good estate, and he gives the reason, because they were more religious than, their neighbours: why

was Israel so often spoiled by their enemies, led into captivity, &c., but
for their idolatry, neglect of God's word, for sacrilege, even for one
Achan's fault? And what shall we except that have such multitudes of
Achans, church robbers, simoniacal patrons, &c., how can they hope to
flourish, that neglect divine duties, that live most part like Epicures?
Other common grievances are generally noxious to a body politic;
alteration of laws and customs, breaking privileges, general oppressions,
seditions, &c., observed by *[477]*Aristotle, Bodin, Boterus, Junius,
Arniscus, &c. I will only point at some of chiefest. *[478]Impotentia
gubernandi, ataxia,* confusion, ill government, which proceeds from
unskilful, slothful, griping, covetous, unjust, rash, or tyrannizing
magistrates, when they are fools, idiots, children, proud, wilful, partial,
indiscreet, oppressors, giddy heads, tyrants, not able or unfit to manage
such offices: *[479]*many noble cities and flourishing kingdoms by that
means are desolate, the whole body groans under such heads, and all
the members must needs be disaffected, as at this day those goodly
provinces in Asia Minor, &c. groan under the burthen of a Turkish
government; and those vast kingdoms of Muscovia, Russia, *[480]*under a
tyrannizing duke. Who ever heard of more civil and rich populous
countries than those of Greece, Asia Minor, abounding with
all *[481]*wealth, multitudes of inhabitants, force, power, splendour and
magnificence? and that miracle of countries, *[482]*the Holy Land, that in
so small a compass of ground could maintain so many towns, cities,
produce so many fighting men? Egypt another paradise, now barbarous
and desert, and almost waste, by the despotical government of an
imperious Turk, *intolerabili servitutis jugo premitur* (*[483]*one saith) not
only fire and water, goods or lands, *sed ipse spiritus ab insolentissimi
victoris pendet nutu,* such is their slavery, their lives and souls depend
upon his insolent will and command. A tyrant that spoils all wheresoever
he comes, insomuch that an *[484]*historian complains, if an old
inhabitant should now see them, he would not know them, if a traveller,
or stranger, it would grieve his heart to behold
them. Whereas *[485]*Aristotle notes, *Novae exactiones, nova onera
imposita,* new burdens and exactions daily come upon them, like those of
which Zosimus, *lib. 2,* so grievous, *ut viri uxores, patres filios
prostituerent ut exactoribus e questu,* &c., they must needs be
discontent, *hinc civitatum gemitus et ploratus,* as *[486]* Tully holds, hence
come those complaints and tears of cities, poor, miserable, rebellious,
and desperate subjects, as *[487]*Hippolitus adds; and *[488]*as a judicious
countryman of ours observed not long since, in a survey of that great
Duchy of Tuscany, the people lived much grieved and discontent, as
appeared by their manifold and manifest complainings in that kind. That
the state was like a sick body which had lately taken physic, whose
humours are not yet well settled, and weakened so much by purging,
that nothing was left but melancholy.
Whereas the princes and potentates are immoderate in lust, hypocrites,
epicures, of no religion, but in show: *Quid hypocrisi fragilius?* what so
brittle and unsure? what sooner subverts their estates than wandering
and raging lusts, on their subjects' wives, daughters? to say no worse.
That they should *facem praeferre,* lead the way to all virtuous actions,

are the ringleaders oftentimes of all mischief and dissolute courses, and by that means their countries are plagued, *[489]*and they themselves often ruined, banished, or murdered by conspiracy of their subjects, as Sardanapalus was, Dionysius Junior, Heliogabalus, Periander, Pisistratus, Tarquinius, Timocrates, Childericus, Appius Claudius, Andronicus, Galeacius Sforza, Alexander Medices, &c. Whereas the princes or great men are malicious, envious, factious, ambitious, emulators, they tear a commonwealth asunder, as so many Guelfs and Gibelines disturb the quietness of it, *[490]*and with mutual murders let it bleed to death; our histories are too full of such barbarous inhumanities, and the miseries that issue from them. Whereas they be like so many horseleeches, hungry, griping, corrupt, *[491]* covetous, *avaritice mancipia,* ravenous as wolves, for as Tully writes: *qui praeest prodest, et qui pecudibus praeest, debet eorum utilitati inservire:* or such as prefer their private before the public good. For as *[492]*he said long since, *res privatae publicis semper officere.* Or whereas they be illiterate, ignorant, empirics in policy, *ubi deest facultas,* *[493]*virtus (Aristot. *pol. 5, cap. 8.*) *et scientia,* wise only by inheritance, and in authority by birthright, favour, or for their wealth and titles; there must needs be a fault, *[494]*a great defect: because as an *[495]*old philosopher affirms, such men are not always fit. Of an infinite number, few alone are senators, and of those few, fewer good, and of that small number of honest, good, and noble men, few that are learned, wise, discreet and sufficient, able to discharge such places, it must needs turn to the confusion of a state. For as the *[496]*Princes are, so are the people; *Qualis Rex, talis grex:* and which *[497]*Antigonus right well said of old, *qui Macedonia regem erudit, omnes etiam subditos erudit,* he that teacheth the king of Macedon, teacheth all his subjects, is a true saying still. For Princes are the glass, the school, the book,

Where subjects' eyes do learn, do read, do look.

———Velocius et citius nos

Corrumpunt vitiorum exempla domestica, magnis

Cum subeant animos auctoribus.———*[498]*

Their examples are soonest followed, vices entertained, if they be profane, irreligious, lascivious, riotous, epicures, factious, covetous, ambitious, illiterate, so will the commons most part be, idle, unthrifts, prone to lust, drunkards, and therefore poor and needy (ἡ πενια στάσιν ἐμποιει καὶ κακουργίαν, for poverty begets sedition and villainy) upon all occasions ready to mutiny and rebel, discontent still, complaining, murmuring, grudging, apt to all outrages, thefts, treasons, murders, innovations, in debt, shifters, cozeners, outlaws, *Profligatae famae ac vitae.* It was an old *[499]*politician's aphorism, They that are poor and bad envy rich, hate good men, abhor the present government, wish for a new, and would

have all turned topsy-turvy. When Catiline rebelled in Rome, he got a
company of such debauched rogues together, they were his familiars and
coadjutors, and such have been your rebels most part in all ages, Jack
Cade, Tom Straw, Kette, and his companions.

Where they be generally riotous and contentious, where there be many
discords, many laws, many lawsuits, many lawyers and many
physicians, it is a manifest sign of a distempered, melancholy state,
as [500]Plato long since maintained: for where such kind of men swarm,
they will make more work for themselves, and that body politic diseased,
which was otherwise sound. A general mischief in these our times, an
insensible plague, and never so many of them: which are now
multiplied (saith Mat. Geraldus, [501]a lawyer himself,) as so many
locusts, not the parents, but the plagues of the country, and for the most
part a supercilious, bad, covetous, litigious generation of
men. [502]Crumenimulga natio &c. A purse-milking nation, a clamorous
company, gowned vultures, [503]qui ex injuria vivent et sanguine civium,
thieves and seminaries of discord; worse than any pollers by the highway
side, auri accipitres, auri exterebronides, pecuniarum hamiolae,
quadruplatores, curiae harpagones, fori tintinabula, monstra hominum,
mangones, &c. that take upon them to make peace, but are indeed the
very disturbers of our peace, a company of irreligious harpies, scraping,
griping catchpoles, (I mean our common hungry
pettifoggers, [504]rabulas forenses, love and honour in the meantime all
good laws, and worthy lawyers, that are so many [505]oracles and pilots
of a well-governed commonwealth). Without art, without judgment, that
do more harm, as [506]Livy said, quam bella externa, fames, morbive,
than sickness, wars, hunger, diseases; and cause a most incredible
destruction of a commonwealth, saith [507]Sesellius, a famous civilian
sometimes in Paris, as ivy doth by an oak, embrace it so long, until it
hath got the heart out of it, so do they by such places they inhabit; no
counsel at all, no justice, no speech to be had, nisi eum premulseris, he
must be fed still, or else he is as mute as a fish, better open an oyster
without a knife. Experto crede (saith [508] Salisburiensis) in manus eorum
millies incidi, et Charon immitis qui nulli pepercit unquam, his longe
clementior est; I speak out of experience, I have been a thousand times
amongst them, and Charon himself is more gentle than they; [509]he is
contented with his single pay, but they multiply still, they are never
satisfied, besides they have damnificas linguas, as he terms it, nisi
funibus argenteis vincias, they must be fed to say nothing, and [510]get
more to hold their peace than we can to say our best. They will speak
their clients fair, and invite them to their tables, but as he follows
it, [511]of all injustice there is none so pernicious as that of theirs, which
when they deceive most, will seem to be honest men. They take upon
them to be peacemakers, et fovere causas humilium, to help them to their
right, patrocinantur afflictis, [512]but all is for their own good, ut loculos
pleniorom exhauriant, they plead for poor men gratis, but they are but as
a stale to catch others. If there be no jar, [513]they can make a jar, out of
the law itself find still some quirk or other, to set them at odds, and
continue causes so long, lustra aliquot, I know not how many years

before the cause is heard, and when 'tis judged and determined by
reason of some tricks and errors, it is as fresh to begin, after twice seven
years sometimes, as it was at first; and so they prolong time, delay suits
till they have enriched themselves, and beggared their clients. And,
as *[514]*Cato inveighed against Isocrates' scholars, we may justly tax our
wrangling lawyers, they do *consenescere in litibus*, are so litigious and
busy here on earth, that I think they will plead their client's causes
hereafter, some of them in hell. *[515]* Simlerus complains amongst the
Swissers of the advocates in his time, that when they should make an
end, they began controversies, and protract their causes many years,
persuading them their title is good, till their patrimonies be consumed,
and that they have spent more in seeking than the thing is worth, or they
shall get by the recovery. So that he that goes to law, as the proverb
is, *[516]*holds a wolf by the ears, or as a sheep in a storm runs for shelter
to a brier, if he prosecute his cause he is consumed, if he surcease his
suit he loseth all; *[517]*what difference? They had wont heretofore, saith
Austin, to end matters, *per communes arbitros*; and so in Switzerland (we
are informed by *[518]*Simlerus), they had some common arbitrators or
daysmen in every town, that made a friendly composition betwixt man
and man, and he much wonders at their honest simplicity, that could
keep peace so well, and end such great causes by that
means. At *[519]*Fez in Africa, they have neither lawyers nor advocates;
but if there be any controversies amongst them, both parties plaintiff and
defendant come to their Alfakins or chief judge, and at once without any
farther appeals or pitiful delays, the cause is heard and ended. Our
forefathers, as *[520]*a worthy chorographer of ours observes, had
wont *pauculis cruculis aureis*, with a few golden crosses, and lines in
verse, make all conveyances, assurances. And such was the candour and
integrity of succeeding ages, that a deed (as I have oft seen) to convey a
whole manor, was *implicite* contained in some twenty lines or
thereabouts; like that scede or *Sytala Laconica*, so much renowned of old
in all contracts, which *[521]*Tully so earnestly commends to Atticus,
Plutarch in his Lysander, Aristotle *polit.*: Thucydides, *lib.*
1, *[522]*Diodorus and Suidus approve and magnify, for that laconic
brevity in this kind; and well they might, for, according
to *[523]*Tertullian, *certa sunt paucis*, there is much more certainty in
fewer words. And so was it of old throughout: but now many skins of
parchment will scarce serve turn; he that buys and sells a house, must
have a house full of writings, there be so many circumstances, so many
words, such tautological repetitions of all particulars (to avoid cavillation
they say); but we find by our woeful experience, that to subtle wits it is a
cause of much more contention and variance, and scarce any conveyance
so accurately penned by one, which another will not find a crack in, or
cavil at; if any one word be misplaced, any little error, all is disannulled.
That which is a law today, is none tomorrow; that which is sound in one
man's opinion, is most faulty to another; that in conclusion, here is
nothing amongst us but contention and confusion, we bandy one against
another. And that which long since *[524]*Plutarch complained of them in
Asia, may be verified in our times. These men here assembled, come not
to sacrifice to their gods, to offer Jupiter their first-fruits, or merriments

to Bacchus; but an yearly disease exasperating Asia hath brought them hither, to make an end of their controversies and lawsuits. 'Tis *multitudo perdentium et pereuntium*, a destructive rout that seek one another's ruin. Such most part are our ordinary suitors, termers, clients, new stirs every day, mistakes, errors, cavils, and at this present, as I have heard in some one court, I know not how many thousand causes: no person free, no title almost good, with such bitterness in following, so many slights, procrastinations, delays, forgery, such cost (for infinite sums are inconsiderately spent), violence and malice, I know not by whose fault, lawyers, clients, laws, both or all: but as Paul reprehended the *[525]*Corinthians long since, I may more positively infer now: There is a fault amongst you, and I speak it to your shame, Is there not a *[526]*wise man amongst you, to judge between his brethren? but that a brother goes to law with a brother. And *[527]*Christ's counsel concerning lawsuits, was never so fit to be inculcated as in this age: *[528]*Agree with thine adversary quickly, &c. Matth. v. 25.

I could repeat many such particular grievances, which must disturb a body politic. To shut up all in brief, where good government is, prudent and wise princes, there all things thrive and prosper, peace and happiness is in that land: where it is otherwise, all things are ugly to behold, incult, barbarous, uncivil, a paradise is turned to a wilderness. This island amongst the rest, our next neighbours the French and Germans, may be a sufficient witness, that in a short time by that prudent policy of the Romans, was brought from barbarism; see but what Caesar reports of us, and Tacitus of those old Germans, they were once as uncivil as they in Virginia, yet by planting of colonies and good laws, they became from barbarous outlaws, *[529]*to be full of rich and populous cities, as now they are, and most flourishing kingdoms. Even so might Virginia, and those wild Irish have been civilised long since, if that order had been heretofore taken, which now begins, of planting colonies, &c. I have read a *[530]*discourse, printed *anno* 1612. Discovering the true causes why Ireland was never entirely subdued, or brought under obedience to the crown of England, until the beginning of his Majesty's happy reign. Yet if his reasons were thoroughly scanned by a judicious politician, I am afraid he would not altogether be approved, but that it would turn to the dishonour of our nation, to suffer it to lie so long waste. Yea, and if some travellers should see (to come nearer home) those rich, united provinces of Holland, Zealand, &c., over against us; those neat cities and populous towns, full of most industrious artificers, *[531]*so much land recovered from the sea, and so painfully preserved by those artificial inventions, so wonderfully approved, as that of Bemster in Holland, *ut nihil huic par aut simile invenias in toto orbe*, saith Bertius the geographer, all the world cannot match it, *[532]*so many navigable channels from place to place, made by men's hands, &c. and on the other side so many thousand acres of our fens lie drowned, our cities thin, and those vile, poor, and ugly to behold in respect of theirs, our trades decayed, our still running rivers stopped, and that beneficial use of transportation, wholly neglected, so many havens void of ships and towns, so many parks and forests for pleasure, barren heaths, so many villages depopulated, &c. I think sure he would find some fault.

I may not deny but that this nation of ours, doth *bene audire apud exteros*, is a most noble, a most flourishing kingdom, by common consent of all *[533]*geographers, historians, politicians, 'tis *unica velut arx*, *[534]*and which Quintius in Livy said of the inhabitants of Peloponnesus, may be well applied to us, we are *testudines testa sua inclusi*, like so many tortoises in our shells, safely defended by an angry sea, as a wall on all sides. Our island hath many such honourable eulogiums; and as a learned countryman of ours right well hath it, *[535]*Ever since the Normans first coming into England, this country both for military matters, and all other of civility, hath been paralleled with the most flourishing kingdoms of Europe and our Christian world, a blessed, a rich country, and one of the fortunate isles: and for some things *[536]*preferred before other countries, for expert seamen, our laborious discoveries, art of navigation, true merchants, they carry the bell away from all other nations, even the Portugals and Hollanders themselves; *[537]*without all fear, saith Boterus, furrowing the ocean winter and summer, and two of their captains, with no less valour than fortune, have sailed round about the world. *[538]* We have besides many particular blessings, which our neighbours want, the Gospel truly preached, church discipline established, long peace and quietness free from exactions, foreign fears, invasions, domestical seditions, well manured, *[539]*fortified by art, and nature, and now most happy in that fortunate union of England and Scotland, which our forefathers have laboured to effect, and desired to see. But in which we excel all others, a wise, learned, religious king, another Numa, a second Augustus, a true Josiah; most worthy senators, a learned clergy, an obedient commonalty, &c. Yet amongst many roses, some thistles grow, some bad weeds and enormities, which much disturb the peace of this body politic, eclipse the honour and glory of it, fit to be rooted out, and with all speed to be reformed.

The first is idleness, by reason of which we have many swarms of rogues, and beggars, thieves, drunkards, and discontented persons (whom Lycurgus in Plutarch calls *morbos reipublicae*, the boils of the commonwealth), many poor people in all our towns. *Civitates ignobiles*, as *[540]*Polydore calls them, base-built cities, inglorious, poor, small, rare in sight, ruinous, and thin of inhabitants. Our land is fertile we may not deny, full of all good things, and why doth it not then abound with cities, as well as Italy, France, Germany, the Low Countries? because their policy hath been otherwise, and we are not so thrifty, circumspect, industrious. Idleness is the *malus genius* of our nation. For as *[541]*Boterus justly argues, fertility of a country is not enough, except art and industry be joined unto it, according to Aristotle, riches are either natural or artificial; natural are good land, fair mines, &c. artificial, are manufactures, coins, &c. Many kingdoms are fertile, but thin of inhabitants, as that Duchy of Piedmont in Italy, which Leander Albertus so much magnifies for corn, wine, fruits, &c., yet nothing near so populous as those which are more barren.*[542]*England, saith he, London only excepted, hath never a populous city, and yet a fruitful country. I find 46 cities and walled towns in Alsatia, a small province in Germany, 50 castles, an infinite number of villages, no ground idle, no not rocky places, or tops of hills are untilled, as *[543]*Munster informeth us. In *[544]*Greichgea, a small territory on the Necker, 24 Italian miles over, I read of 20 walled towns, innumerable villages, each one containing 150 houses most part, besides castles and noblemen's palaces. I observe in *[545]*Turinge in Dutchland (twelve miles over by their scale) 12 counties, and in them 144 cities, 2000 villages, 144 towns, 250 castles. In *[546]*Bavaria 34 cities, 46 towns, &c. *[547]*Portugallia interamnis, a small plot of ground, hath 1460 parishes, 130 monasteries, 200 bridges. Malta, a barren island, yields 20,000 inhabitants. But of all the rest, I admire Lues Guicciardine's relations of the Low Countries. Holland hath 26 cities, 400 great villages. Zealand 10 cities, 102 parishes. Brabant 26 cities, 102 parishes. Flanders 28 cities, 90 towns, 1154 villages, besides abbeys, castles, &c. The Low Countries generally have three cities at least for one of ours, and those far more populous and rich: and what is the cause, but their industry and excellency in all manner of trades? Their commerce, which is maintained by a multitude of tradesmen, so many excellent channels made by art and opportune havens, to which they build their cities; all which we have in like measure, or at least may have. But their chiefest loadstone which draws all manner of commerce and merchandise, which maintains their present estate, is not fertility of soil, but industry that enricheth them, the gold mines of Peru, or Nova Hispania may not compare with them. They have neither gold nor silver of their own, wine nor oil, or scarce any corn growing in those united provinces, little or no wood, tin, lead, iron, silk, wool, any stuff almost, or metal; and yet Hungary, Transylvania, that brag of their mines, fertile England cannot compare with them. I dare boldly say, that neither France, Tarentum, Apulia, Lombardy, or any part of Italy, Valentia in Spain, or that pleasant Andalusia, with their excellent fruits, wine and oil, two harvests, no not any part of Europe is so flourishing, so rich, so populous, so full of good ships, of well-built cities, so abounding with all things necessary for the use of man. 'Tis our Indies, an epitome of China, and all by reason of their industry, good policy, and commerce. Industry is a loadstone to draw all good things; that alone makes countries flourish, cities populous, *[548]*and will enforce by reason of much manure, which necessarily follows, a barren soil to be fertile and good, as sheep, saith *[549]*Dion, mend a bad pasture.

Tell me politicians, why is that fruitful Palestina, noble Greece, Egypt, Asia Minor, so much decayed, and (mere carcases now) fallen from that they were? The ground is the same, but the government is altered, the people are grown slothful, idle, their good husbandry, policy, and industry is decayed. *Non fatigata aut effaeta, humus*, as *[550]*Columella well informs Sylvinus, *sed nostra fit inertia*, &c. May a man believe that which Aristotle in his politics, Pausanias, Stephanus, Sophianus, Gerbelius relate of old Greece? I find heretofore 70 cities in Epirus overthrown by Paulus Aemilius, a goodly province in times past, *[551]*now left desolate of good towns and almost inhabitants. Sixty-two cities in Macedonia in Strabo's time. I find 30 in Laconia, but now

scarce so many villages, saith Gerbelius. If any man from Mount
Taygetus should view the country round about, and see *tot delicias, tot
urbes per Peloponesum dispersas*, so many delicate and brave built cities
with such cost and exquisite cunning, so neatly set out in
Peloponnesus, *[552]*he should perceive them now ruinous and
overthrown, burnt, waste, desolate, and laid level with the
ground. *Incredibile dictu*, &c. And as he laments, *Quis talia fando
Temperet a lachrymis? Quis tam durus aut ferreus*, (so he prosecutes
it). *[553]*Who is he that can sufficiently condole and commiserate these
ruins? Where are those 4000 cities of Egypt, those 100 cities in Crete?
Are they now come to two? What saith Pliny and Aelian of old Italy?
There were in former ages 1166 cities: Blondus and Machiavel, both
grant them now nothing near so populous, and full of good towns as in
the time of Augustus (for now Leander Albertus can find but 300 at
most), and if we may give credit to *[554]*Livy, not then so strong and
puissant as of old: They mustered 70 Legions in former times, which now
the known world will scarce yield. Alexander built 70 cities in a short
space for his part, our sultans and Turks demolish twice as many, and
leave all desolate. Many will not believe but that our island of Great
Britain is now more populous than ever it was; yet let them read Bede,
Leland and others, they shall find it most flourished in the Saxon
Heptarchy, and in the Conqueror's time was far better inhabited, than at
this present. See that Doomsday Book, and show me those thousands of
parishes, which are now decayed, cities ruined, villages depopulated, &c.
The lesser the territory is, commonly, the richer it is. *Parvus sed bene
cultus ager*. As those Athenian, Lacedaemonian, Arcadian, Aelian,
Sycionian, Messenian, &c. commonwealths of Greece make ample proof,
as those imperial cities and free states of Germany may witness, those
Cantons of Switzers, Rheti, Grisons, Walloons, Territories of Tuscany,
Luke and Senes of old, Piedmont, Mantua, Venice in Italy, Ragusa, &c.
That prince therefore as, *[555]*Boterus adviseth, that will have a rich
country, and fair cities, let him get good trades, privileges, painful
inhabitants, artificers, and suffer no rude matter unwrought, as tin, iron,
wool, lead, &c., to be transported out of his country,—*[556]*a thing in
part seriously attempted amongst us, but not effected. And because
industry of men, and multitude of trade so much avails to the ornament
and enriching of a kingdom; those ancient *[557]*Massilians would admit
no man into their city that had not some trade. Selym the first Turkish
emperor procured a thousand good artificers to be brought from Tauris
to Constantinople. The Polanders indented with Henry Duke of Anjou,
their new chosen king, to bring with him an hundred families of artificers
into Poland. James the first in Scotland (as *[558]*Buchanan writes) sent
for the best artificers he could get in Europe, and gave them great
rewards to teach his subjects their several trades. Edward the Third, our
most renowned king, to his eternal memory, brought clothing first into
this island, transporting some families of artificers from Gaunt hither.
How many goodly cities could I reckon up, that thrive wholly by trade,
where thousands of inhabitants live singular well by their fingers' ends:
As Florence in Italy by making cloth of gold; great Milan by silk, and all
curious works; Arras in Artois by those fair hangings; many cities in

Spain, many in France, Germany, have none other maintenance, especially those within the land. *[559]*Mecca, in Arabia Petraea, stands in a most unfruitful country, that wants water, amongst the rocks (as Vertomannus describes it), and yet it is a most elegant and pleasant city, by reason of the traffic of the east and west. Ormus in Persia is a most famous mart-town, hath nought else but the opportunity of the haven to make it flourish. Corinth, a noble city (Lumen Greciae, Tully calls it) the Eye of Greece, by reason of Cenchreas and Lecheus, those excellent ports, drew all that traffic of the Ionian and Aegean seas to it; and yet the country about it was *curva et superciliosa*, as *[560]*Strabo terms it, rugged and harsh. We may say the same of Athens, Actium, Thebes, Sparta, and most of those towns in Greece. Nuremberg in Germany is sited in a most barren soil, yet a noble imperial city, by the sole industry of artificers, and cunning trades, they draw the riches of most countries to them, so expert in manufactures, that as Sallust long since gave out of the like, *Sedem animae in extremis digitis habent*, their soul, or *intellectus agens*, was placed in their fingers' end; and so we may say of Basil, Spire, Cambray, Frankfurt, &c. It is almost incredible to speak what some write of Mexico and the cities adjoining to it, no place in the world at their first discovery more populous, *[561]*Mat. Riccius, the Jesuit, and some others, relate of the industry of the Chinese most populous countries, not a beggar or an idle person to be seen, and how by that means they prosper and flourish. We have the same means, able bodies, pliant wits, matter of all sorts, wool, flax, iron, tin, lead, wood, &c., many excellent subjects to work upon, only industry is wanting. We send our best commodities beyond the seas, which they make good use of to their necessities, set themselves a work about, and severally improve, sending the same to us back at dear rates, or else make toys and baubles of the tails of them, which they sell to us again, at as great a reckoning as the whole. In most of our cities, some few excepted, like *[562]*Spanish loiterers, we live wholly by tippling-inns and alehouses. Malting are their best ploughs, their greatest traffic to sell ale. *[563]*Meteran and some others object to us, that we are no whit so industrious as the Hollanders: Manual trades (saith he) which are more curious or troublesome, are wholly exercised by strangers: they dwell in a sea full of fish, but they are so idle, they will not catch so much as shall serve their own turns, but buy it of their neighbours. Tush *[564]*Mare liberum, they fish under our noses, and sell it to us when they have done, at their own prices.

————Pudet haec opprobria nobis

Et dici potuisse, et non potuisse refelli.

I am ashamed to hear this objected by strangers, and know not how to answer it.

Amongst our towns, there is only *[565]*London that bears the face of a city, *[566]Epitome Britanniae*, a famous emporium, second to none beyond seas, a noble mart: but *sola crescit, decrescentibus aliis*; and yet, in my slender judgment, defective in many things. The rest (*[567]*some few excepted) are in mean estate, ruinous most part, poor, and full of beggars, by reason of their decayed trades, neglected or bad policy, idleness of their inhabitants, riot, which had rather beg or loiter, and be ready to starve, than work.

I cannot deny but that something may be said in defence of our cities, *[568]*that they are not so fair built, (for the sole magnificence of this kingdom (concerning buildings) hath been of old in those Norman castles and religious houses,) so rich, thick sited, populous, as in some other countries; besides the reasons Cardan gives, *Subtil. Lib. 11.* we want wine and oil, their two harvests, we dwell in a colder air, and for that cause must a little more liberally *[569]*feed of flesh, as all northern countries do: our provisions will not therefore extend to the maintenance of so many; yet notwithstanding we have matter of all sorts, an open sea for traffic, as well as the rest, goodly havens. And how can we excuse our negligence, our riot, drunkenness, &c., and such enormities that follow it? We have excellent laws enacted, you will say, severe statutes, houses of correction, &c., to small purpose it seems; it is not houses will serve, but cities of correction; *[570]*our trades generally ought to be reformed, wants supplied. In other countries they have the same grievances, I confess, but that doth not excuse us, *[571]*wants, defects, enormities, idle drones, tumults, discords, contention, lawsuits, many laws made against them to repress those innumerable brawls and lawsuits, excess in apparel, diet, decay of tillage, depopulations, *[572]*especially against rogues, beggars, Egyptian vagabonds (so termed at least) which have *[573]* swarmed all over Germany, France, Italy, Poland, as you may read in *[574]* Munster, Cranzius, and Aventinus; as those Tartars and Arabians at this day do in the eastern countries: yet such has been the iniquity of all ages, as it seems to small purpose. *Nemo in nostra civitate mendicus esto, [575]* saith Plato: he will have them purged from a *[576]*commonwealth, *[577]*as a bad humour from the body, that are like so many ulcers and boils, and must be cured before the melancholy body can be eased.

What Carolus Magnus, the Chinese, the Spaniards, the duke of Saxony and many other states have decreed in this case, read Arniseus, *cap. 19*; Boterus, *libro 8, cap. 2*; Osorius *de Rubus gest. Eman. lib. 11.* When a country is overstocked with people, as a pasture is oft overlaid with cattle, they had wont in former times to disburden themselves, by sending out colonies, or by wars, as those old Romans; or by employing them at home about some public buildings, as bridges, roadways, for which those Romans were famous in this island; as Augustus Caesar did in Rome, the Spaniards in their Indian mines, as at Potosi in Peru, where some 30,000 men are still at work, 6000 furnaces ever boiling, &c. *[578]*aqueducts, bridges, havens, those stupend works of Trajan, Claudius, at *[579]*Ostium, Dioclesiani Therma, Fucinus Lacus, that Piraeum in Athens, made by Themistocles, ampitheatrums of curious marble, as at Verona, Civitas Philippi, and Heraclea in Thrace, those Appian and Flaminian ways, prodigious works all may witness; and rather than they should be *[580]*idle, as those *[581]* Egyptian Pharaohs, Maris, and Sesostris did, to task their subjects to build unnecessary pyramids, obelisks, labyrinths, channels, lakes, gigantic works all, to

divert them from rebellion, riot, drunkenness, *[582]Quo scilicet alantur et ne vagando laborare desuescant.*
Another eyesore is that want of conduct and navigable rivers, a great blemish as *[583]*Boterus, *[584]*Hippolitus a Collibus, and other politicians hold, if it be neglected in a commonwealth. Admirable cost and charge is bestowed in the Low Countries on this behalf, in the duchy of Milan, territory of Padua, in *[585]*France, Italy, China, and so likewise about corrivations of water to moisten and refresh barren grounds, to drain fens, bogs, and moors. Massinissa made many inward parts of Barbary and Numidia in Africa, before his time incult and horrid, fruitful and bartable by this means. Great industry is generally used all over the eastern countries in this kind, especially in Egypt, about Babylon and Damascus, as Vertomannus and *[586]*Gotardus Arthus relate; about Barcelona, Segovia, Murcia, and many other places of Spain, Milan in Italy; by reason of which, their soil is much impoverished, and infinite commodities arise to the inhabitants.
The Turks of late attempted to cut that Isthmus betwixt Africa and Asia, which *[587]*Sesostris and Darius, and some Pharaohs of Egypt had formerly undertaken, but with ill success, as *[588]*Diodorus Siculus records, and Pliny, for that Red Sea being three *[589]*cubits higher than Egypt, would have drowned all the country, *caepto destiterant,* they left off; yet as the same *[590]*Diodorus writes, Ptolemy renewed the work many years after, and absolved in it a more opportune place.
That Isthmus of Corinth was likewise undertaken to be made navigable by Demetrius, by Julius Caesar, Nero, Domitian, Herodes Atticus, to make a speedy *[591]*passage, and less dangerous, from the Ionian and Aegean seas; but because it could not be so well effected, the Peloponnesians built a wall like our Picts' wall about Schaenute, where Neptune's temple stood, and in the shortest cut over the Isthmus, of which Diodorus, *lib. 11.* Herodotus, *lib. 8. Uran.* Our latter writers call it Hexamilium, which Amurath the Turk demolished, the Venetians, *anno* 1453, repaired in 15 days with 30,000 men. Some, saith Acosta, would have a passage cut from Panama to Nombre de Dios in America; but Thuanus and Serres the French historians speak of a famous aqueduct in France, intended in Henry the Fourth's time, from the Loire to the Seine, and from Rhodanus to the Loire. The like to which was formerly assayed by Domitian the emperor, *[592]*from Arar to Moselle, which Cornelius Tacitus speaks of in the 13 of his annals, after by Charles the Great and others. Much cost hath in former times been bestowed in either new making or mending channels of rivers, and their passages, (as Aurelianus did by Tiber to make it navigable to Rome, to convey corn from Egypt to the city, *vadum alvei tumentis effodit* saith Vopiscus, *et Tiberis ripas extruxit* he cut fords, made banks, &c.) decayed havens, which Claudius the emperor with infinite pains and charges attempted at Ostia, as I have said, the Venetians at this day to preserve their city; many excellent means to enrich their territories, have been fostered, invented in most provinces of Europe, as planting some Indian plants amongst us, silkworms, *[593]*the very mulberry leaves in the plains of Granada yield 30,000 crowns per annum to the king of Spain's coffers, besides those many trades and artificers that are busied about

them in the kingdom of Granada, Murcia, and all over Spain. In France a
great benefit is raised by salt, &c., whether these things might not be as
happily attempted with us, and with like success, it may be controverted,
silkworms (I mean) vines, fir trees, &c. Cardan exhorts Edward the Sixth
to plant olives, and is fully persuaded they would prosper in this island.
With us, navigable rivers are most part neglected; our streams are not
great, I confess, by reason of the narrowness of the island, yet they run
smoothly and even, not headlong, swift, or amongst rocks and shelves,
as foaming Rhodanus and Loire in France, Tigris in Mesopotamia, violent
Durius in Spain, with cataracts and whirlpools, as the Rhine, and
Danubius, about Shaffausen, Lausenburgh, Linz, and Cremmes, to
endanger navigators; or broad shallow, as Neckar in the Palatinate,
Tibris in Italy; but calm and fair as Arar in France, Hebrus in Macedonia,
Eurotas in Laconia, they gently glide along, and might as well be repaired
many of them (I mean Wye, Trent, Ouse, Thamisis at Oxford, the defect
of which we feel in the mean time) as the river of Lee from Ware to
London. B. Atwater of old, or as some will Henry I. *[594]*made a channel
from Trent to Lincoln, navigable; which now, saith Mr. Camden, is
decayed, and much mention is made of anchors, and such like
monuments found about old *[595]*Verulamium, good ships have formerly
come to Exeter, and many such places, whose channels, havens, ports
are now barred and rejected. We contemn this benefit of carriage by
waters, and are therefore compelled in the inner parts of this island,
because portage is so dear, to eat up our commodities ourselves, and live
like so many boars in a sty, for want of vent and utterance.
We have many excellent havens, royal havens, Falmouth, Portsmouth,
Milford, &c. equivalent if not to be preferred to that Indian Havana, old
Brundusium in Italy, Aulis in Greece, Ambracia in Acarnia, Suda in
Crete, which have few ships in them, little or no traffic or trade, which
have scarce a village on them, able to bear great cities, *sed viderint
politici*. I could here justly tax many other neglects, abuses, errors,
defects among us, and in other countries, depopulations, riot,
drunkenness, &c. and many such, *quae nunc in aurem susurrare, non
libet*. But I must take heed, *ne quid gravius dicam*, that I do not
overshoot myself, *Sus Minervam*, I am forth of my element, as you
peradventure suppose; and sometimes *veritas odium parit*, as he
said, verjuice and oatmeal is good for a parrot. For as Lucian said of an
historian, I say of a politician. He that will freely speak and write, must
be for ever no subject, under no prince or law, but lay out the matter
truly as it is, not caring what any can, will, like or dislike.
We have good laws, I deny not, to rectify such enormities, and so in all
other countries, but it seems not always to good purpose. We had need of
some general visitor in our age, that should reform what is amiss; a just
army of Rosy-cross men, for they will amend all matters (they say)
religion, policy, manners, with arts, sciences, &c. Another Attila,
Tamerlane, Hercules, to strive with Achelous, *Augeae stabulum purgare*,
to subdue tyrants, as *[596]*he did Diomedes and Busiris: to expel thieves,
as he did Cacus and Lacinius: to vindicate poor captives, as he did
Hesione: to pass the torrid zone, the deserts of Libya, and purge the
world of monsters and Centaurs: or another Theban Crates to reform our

manners, to compose quarrels and controversies, as in his time he did, and was therefore adored for a god in Athens. As Hercules *[597]*purged the world of monsters, and subdued them, so did he fight against envy, lust, anger, avarice, &c. and all those feral vices and monsters of the mind. It were to be wished we had some such visitor, or if wishing would serve, one had such a ring or rings, as Timolaus desired in *[598]*Lucian, by virtue of which he should be as strong as 10,000 men, or an army of giants, go invisible, open gates and castle doors, have what treasure he would, transport himself in an instant to what place he desired, alter affections, cure all manner of diseases, that he might range over the world, and reform all distressed states and persons, as he would himself. He might reduce those wandering Tartars in order, that infest China on the one side, Muscovy, Poland, on the other; and tame the vagabond Arabians that rob and spoil those eastern countries, that they should never use more caravans, or janissaries to conduct them. He might root out barbarism out of America, and fully discover *Terra Australis Incognita*, find out the north-east and north-west passages, drain those mighty Maeotian fens, cut down those vast Hircinian woods, irrigate those barren Arabian deserts, &c. cure us of our epidemical diseases, *scorbutum, plica, morbus Neapolitanus*, &c. end all our idle controversies, cut off our tumultuous desires, inordinate lusts, root out atheism, impiety, heresy, schism and superstition, which now so crucify the world, catechise gross ignorance, purge Italy of luxury and riot, Spain of superstition and jealousy, Germany of drunkenness, all our northern country of gluttony and intemperance, castigate our hard-hearted parents, masters, tutors; lash disobedient children, negligent servants, correct these spendthrifts and prodigal sons, enforce idle persons to work, drive drunkards off the alehouse, repress thieves, visit corrupt and tyrannizing magistrates, &c. But as L. Licinius taxed Timolaus, you may us. These are vain, absurd and ridiculous wishes not to be hoped: all must be as it is, *[599]*Bocchalinus may cite commonwealths to come before Apollo, and seek to reform the world itself by commissioners, but there is no remedy, it may not be redressed, *desinent homines tum demum stultescere quando esse desinent*, so long as they can wag their beards, they will play the knaves and fools.

Because, therefore, it is a thing so difficult, impossible, and far beyond Hercules labours to be performed; let them be rude, stupid, ignorant, incult, *lapis super lapidem sedeat*, and as the *[600]*apologist will, *resp. tussi, et graveolentia laboret, mundus vitio*, let them be barbarous as they are, let them *[601]*tyrannise, epicurise, oppress, luxuriate, consume themselves with factions, superstitions, lawsuits, wars and contentions, live in riot, poverty, want, misery; rebel, wallow as so many swine in their own dung, with Ulysses' companions, *stultos jubeo esse libenter*. I will yet, to satisfy and please myself, make an Utopia of mine own, a new Atlantis, a poetical commonwealth of mine own, in which I will freely domineer, build cities, make laws, statutes, as I list myself. And why may I not?—*[602]Pictoribus atque poetis*, &c. You know what liberty poets ever had, and besides, my predecessor Democritus was a politician, a recorder of Abdera, a law maker as some say; and why may not I presume so much as he did? Howsoever I will adventure. For the site, if you will needs urge me to it, I am not fully resolved, it may be in *Terra Australi Incognita*, there is room enough (for of my knowledge neither that hungry Spaniard, *[603]*nor Mercurius Britannicus, have yet discovered half of it) or else one of these floating islands in Mare del Zur, which like the Cyanian isles in the Euxine sea, alter their place, and are accessible only at set times, and to some few persons; or one of the fortunate isles, for who knows yet where, or which they are? there is room enough in the inner parts of America, and northern coasts of Asia. But I will choose a site, whose latitude shall be 45 degrees (I respect not minutes) in the midst of the temperate zone, or perhaps under the equator, that *[604]*paradise of the world, *ubi semper virens laurus*, &c. where is a perpetual spring: the longitude for some reasons I will conceal. Yet be it known to all men by these presents, that if any honest gentleman will send in so much money, as Cardan allows an astrologer for casting a nativity, he shall be a sharer, I will acquaint him with my project, or if any worthy man will stand for any temporal or spiritual office or dignity, (for as he said of his archbishopric of Utopia, 'tis *sanctus ambitus*, and not amiss to be sought after,) it shall be freely given without all intercessions, bribes, letters, &c. his own worth shall be the best spokesman; and because we shall admit of no deputies or advowsons, if he be sufficiently qualified, and as able as willing to execute the place himself, be shall have present possession. It shall be divided into 12 or 13 provinces, and those by hills, rivers, roadways, or some more eminent limits exactly bounded. Each province shall have a metropolis, which shall be so placed as a centre almost in a circumference, and the rest at equal distances, some 12 Italian miles asunder, or thereabout, and in them shall be sold all things necessary for the use of man; *statis horis et diebus*, no market towns, markets or fairs, for they do but beggar cities (no village shall stand above 6, 7, or 8 miles from a city) except those emporiums which are by the sea side, general staples, marts, as Antwerp, Venice, Bergen of old, London, &c. cities most part shall be situated upon navigable rivers or lakes, creeks, havens; and for their form, regular, round, square, or long square, *[605]*with fair, broad, and straight *[606]*streets, houses uniform, built of brick and stone, like Bruges, Brussels, Rhegium Lepidi, Berne in Switzerland, Milan, Mantua, Crema, Cambalu in Tartary, described by M. Polus, or that Venetian Palma. I will admit very few or no suburbs, and those of baser building, walls only to keep out man and horse, except it be in some frontier towns, or by the sea side, and those to be fortified *[607]* after the latest manner of fortification, and situated upon convenient havens, or opportune places. In every so built city, I will have convenient churches, and separate places to bury the dead in, not in churchyards; a*citadella* (in some, not all) to command it, prisons for offenders, opportune market places of all sorts, for corn, meat, cattle, fuel, fish, commodious courts of justice, public halls for all societies, bourses, meeting places, armouries, *[608]*in which shall be kept engines for quenching of fire, artillery gardens, public walks, theatres, and spacious fields allotted for all gymnastic sports, and honest recreations, hospitals of all kinds, for children, orphans, old folks, sick men, mad men, soldiers, pest-houses, &c. not built *precario*, or by gouty benefactors, who, when by fraud and rapine they have extorted all their lives, oppressed whole provinces, societies, &c. give something to pious uses, build a satisfactory alms-house, school or bridge, &c. at their last end, or before perhaps, which is no otherwise than to steal a goose, and stick down a feather, rob a thousand to relieve ten; and those hospitals so built and maintained, not by collections, benevolences, donaries, for a set number, (as in ours,) just so many and no more at such a rate, but for all those who stand in need, be they more or less, and that *ex publico aerario*, and so still maintained, *non nobis solum nati sumus*, &c. I will have conduits of sweet and good water, aptly disposed in each town, common *[609]* granaries, as at Dresden in Misnia, Stetein in Pomerland, Noremberg, &c. Colleges of mathematicians, musicians, and actors, as of old at Labedum in Ionia, *[610]*alchemists, physicians, artists, and philosophers: that all arts and sciences may sooner be perfected and better learned; and public historiographers, as amongst those ancient *[611]*Persians, *qui in commentarios referebant quae memoratu digna gerebantur*, informed and appointed by the state to register all famous acts, and not by each insufficient scribbler, partial or parasitical pedant, as in our times. I will provide public schools of all kinds, singing, dancing, fencing, &c. especially of grammar and languages, not to be taught by those tedious precepts ordinarily used, but by use, example, conversation, *[612]*as travellers learn abroad, and nurses teach their children: as I will have all such places, so will I ordain *[613]*public governors, fit officers to each place, treasurers, aediles, quaestors, overseers of pupils, widows' goods, and all public houses, &c. and those once a year to make strict accounts of all receipts, expenses, to avoid confusion, *et sic fiet ut non absumant* (as Pliny to Trajan,) *quad pudeat dicere*. They shall be subordinate to those higher officers and governors of each city, which shall not be poor tradesmen, and mean artificers, but noblemen and gentlemen, which shall be tied to residence in those towns they dwell next, at such set times and seasons: for I see no reason (which *[614]*Hippolitus complains of) that it should be more dishonourable for noblemen to govern the city than the country, or unseemly to dwell there now, than of old. *[615]*I will have no bogs, fens, marshes, vast woods, deserts, heaths, commons, but all enclosed; (yet not depopulated, and therefore take heed you mistake me not) for that which is common, and every man's, is no man's; the richest countries are still enclosed, as Essex, Kent, with us, &c. Spain, Italy; and where enclosures are least in quantity, they are best *[616]*husbanded, as about Florence in Italy, Damascus in Syria, &c. which are liker gardens than fields. I will not have a barren acre in all my territories, not so much as the tops of mountains: where nature fails, it shall be supplied by art: *[617]*lakes and rivers shall not be left desolate. All common highways, bridges, banks, corrivations of waters, aqueducts, channels, public works, buildings, &c. out of a *[618]*common stock, curiously maintained and kept in repair; no depopulations, engrossings, alterations of wood, arable, but by the consent of some supervisors that shall be appointed for that purpose, to see what reformation ought to be had in all places, what is amiss, how to help it, *et quid quaeque ferat regio, et quid quaeque recuset*, what ground is aptest for wood, what for corn, what for cattle, gardens, orchards, fishponds, &c. with a charitable division in every village, (not one domineering house greedily to swallow up all, which is too common with us) what for lords,*[619]*what for tenants; and because they shall be better encouraged to improve such lands they hold, manure, plant trees, drain, fence, &c. they shall have long leases, a known rent, and known fine to free them from those intolerable exactions of tyrannizing landlords. These supervisors shall likewise appoint what quantity of land in each manor is fit for the lord's demesnes, *[620]*what for holding of tenants, how it ought to be husbanded, *ut [621]magnetis equis, Minyae gens cognita remis*, how to be manured, tilled, rectified, *[622]hic segetes veniunt, illic felicius uvae, arborei foetus alibi, atque injussa virescunt Gramina*, and what proportion is fit for all callings, because private professors are many times idiots, ill husbands, oppressors, covetous, and know not how to improve their own, or else wholly respect their own, and not public good.

Utopian parity is a kind of government, to be wished for, *[623]*rather than effected, *Respub. Christianopolitana*, Campanella's city of the Sun, and that new Atlantis, witty fictions, but mere chimeras; and Plato's community in many things is impious, absurd and ridiculous, it takes away all splendour and magnificence. I will have several orders, degrees of nobility, and those hereditary, not rejecting younger brothers in the mean time, for they shall be sufficiently provided for by pensions, or so qualified, brought up in some honest calling, they shall be able to live of themselves. I will have such a proportion of ground belonging to every barony, he that buys the land shall buy the barony, he that by riot consumes his patrimony, and ancient demesnes, shall forfeit his honours. *[624]*As some dignities shall be hereditary, so some again by election, or by gift (besides free officers, pensions, annuities,) like our bishoprics, prebends, the Bassa's palaces in Turkey, the *[625]*procurator's houses and offices in Venice, which, like the golden apple, shall be given to the worthiest, and best deserving both in war and peace, as a reward of their worth and good service, as so many goals for all to aim at, (*honos alit artes*) and encouragements to others. For I hate these severe, unnatural, harsh, German, French, and Venetian decrees, which exclude plebeians from honours, be they never so wise, rich, virtuous, valiant, and well qualified, they must not be patricians, but keep their own rank, this is *naturae bellum inferre*, odious to God and men, I abhor it. My form of government shall be monarchical. *[626]*nunquam libertas gratior extat,

Quam sub Rege pio, &c.

few laws, but those severely kept, plainly put down, and in the mother tongue, that every man may understand. Every city shall have a peculiar trade or privilege, by which it shall be chiefly maintained: *[627]*and parents shall teach their children one of three at least, bring up and instruct them in the mysteries of their own trade. In each town these several tradesmen shall be so aptly disposed, as they shall free the rest from danger or offence: fire-trades, as smiths, forge-men, brewers, bakers, metal-men, &c., shall dwell apart by themselves: dyers, tanners, fellmongers, and such as use water in convenient places by themselves: noisome or fulsome for bad smells, as butchers' slaughterhouses, chandlers, curriers, in remote places, and some back lanes. Fraternities and companies, I approve of, as merchants' bourses, colleges of druggists, physicians, musicians, &c., but all trades to be rated in the sale of wares, as our clerks of the market do bakers and brewers; corn itself, what scarcity soever shall come, not to extend such a price. Of such wares as are transported or brought in, *[628]*if they be necessary, commodious, and such as nearly concern man's life, as corn, wood, coal, &c., and such provision we cannot want, I will have little or no custom paid, no taxes; but for such things as are for pleasure, delight, or ornament, as wine, spice, tobacco, silk, velvet, cloth of gold, lace, jewels, &c., a greater impost. I will have certain ships sent out for new discoveries every year, *[629]*and some discreet men appointed to travel into all neighbouring kingdoms by land, which shall observe what artificial inventions and good laws are in other countries, customs, alterations, or aught else, concerning war or peace, which may tend to the common good. Ecclesiastical discipline, *penes Episcopos*, subordinate as the other. No impropriations, no lay patrons of church livings, or one private man, but common societies, corporations, &c., and those rectors of benefices to be chosen out of the Universities, examined and approved, as the literati in China. No parish to contain above a thousand auditors. If it were possible, I would have such priest as should imitate Christ, charitable lawyers should love their neighbours as themselves, temperate and modest physicians, politicians contemn the world, philosophers should know themselves, noblemen live honestly, tradesmen leave lying and cozening, magistrates corruption, &c., but this is impossible, I must get such as I may. I will therefore have *[630]*of lawyers, judges, advocates, physicians, chirurgeons, &c., a set number, *[631]*and every man, if it be possible, to plead his own cause, to tell that tale to the judge which he doth to his advocate, as at Fez in Africa, Bantam, Aleppo, Ragusa, *suam quisque causam dicere tenetur*. Those advocates, chirurgeons, and *[632]*physicians, which are allowed to be maintained out of the *[633]*common treasury, no fees to be given or taken upon pain of losing their places; or if they do, very small fees, and when the *[634]*cause is fully ended. *[635]*He that sues any man shall put in a pledge, which if it be proved he hath wrongfully sued his adversary, rashly or maliciously, he shall forfeit, and lose. Or else before any suit begin, the plaintiff shall have his complaint approved by a set delegacy to that purpose; if it be of moment he shall be suffered as before, to proceed, if otherwise they shall determine it. All causes shall be pleaded *suppresso nomine*, the parties' names concealed, if some circumstances do not otherwise require. Judges and other officers shall be aptly disposed in each province, villages, cities, as common arbitrators to hear causes, and end all controversies, and those not single, but three at least on the bench at once, to determine or give sentence, and those again to sit by turns or lots, and not to continue still in the same office. No controversy to depend above a year, but without all delays and further appeals to be speedily despatched, and finally concluded in that time allotted. These and all other inferior magistrates to be chosen *[636]*as the literati in China, or by those exact suffrages of the *[637]*Venetians, and such again not to be eligible, or capable of magistracies, honours, offices, except they be sufficiently *[638]*qualified for learning, manners, and that by the strict approbation of deputed examiners: *[639]*first scholars to take place, then soldiers; for I am of Vigetius his opinion, a scholar deserves better than a soldier, because *Unius aetatis sunt quae fortiter fiunt, quae vero pro utilitate Reipub. scribuntur, aeterna*: a soldier's work lasts for an age, a scholar's for ever. If they *[640]*misbehave themselves, they shall be deposed, and accordingly punished, and whether their offices be annual *[641]*or otherwise, once a year they shall be called in question, and give an account; for men are partial and passionate, merciless, covetous, corrupt, subject to love, hate, fear, favour, &c., *omne sub regno graviore regnum*: like Solon's Areopagites, or those Roman Censors, some shall visit others, and *[642]*be visited *invicem* themselves, *[643]* they shall oversee that no prowling officer, under colour of authority, shall insult over his inferiors, as so many wild beasts, oppress, domineer, flea, grind, or trample on, be partial or corrupt, but that there be *aequabile jus*, justice equally done, live as friends and brethren together; and which *[644]*Sesellius would have and so much desires in his kingdom of France, a diapason and sweet harmony of kings, princes, nobles, and plebeians so mutually tied and involved in love, as well as laws and authority, as that they never disagree, insult, or encroach one upon another. If any man deserve well in his office he shall be rewarded.

————quis enim virtutem amplectitur ipsam,

Proemia si tollas?————*[645]*

He that invents anything for public good in any art or science, writes a treatise, *[646]*or performs any noble exploit, at home or abroad, *[647]* shall be accordingly enriched, *[648]*honoured, and preferred. I say with Hannibal in Ennius, *Hostem qui feriet erit mihi Carthaginensis*, let him be of what condition he will, in all offices, actions, he that deserves best shall have best.

Tilianus in Philonius, out of a charitable mind no doubt, wished all his books were gold and silver, jewels and precious stones, *[649]*to redeem

captives, set free prisoners, and relieve all poor distressed souls that
wanted means; religiously done. I deny not, but to what purpose?
Suppose this were so well done, within a little after, though a man had
Croesus' wealth to bestow, there would be as many more. Wherefore I
will suffer no *[650]*beggars, rogues, vagabonds, or idle persons at all, that
cannot give an account of their lives how they *[651]*maintain themselves.
If they be impotent, lame, blind, and single, they shall be sufficiently
maintained in several hospitals, built for that purpose; if married and
infirm, past work, or by inevitable loss, or some such like misfortune cast
behind, by distribution of *[652]*corn, house-rent free, annual pensions or
money, they shall be relieved, and highly rewarded for their good service
they have formerly done; if able, they shall be enforced to work. *[653]*For
I see no reason (as *[654]*he said) why an epicure or idle drone, a rich
glutton, a usurer, should live at ease, and do nothing, live in honour, in
all manner of pleasures, and oppress others, when as in the meantime a
poor labourer, a smith, a carpenter, an husbandman that hath spent his
time in continual labour, as an ass to carry burdens, to do the
commonwealth good, and without whom we cannot live, shall be left in
his old age to beg or starve, and lead a miserable life worse than a
jument. As *[655]*all conditions shall be tied to their task, so none shall be
overtired, but have their set times of recreations and holidays, *indulgere
genio*, feasts and merry meetings, even to the meanest artificer, or basest
servant, once a week to sing or dance, (though not all at once) or do
whatsoever he shall please; like *[656]*that *Saccarum festum* amongst the
Persians, those Saturnals in Rome, as well as his master. *[657]*If any be
drunk, he shall drink no more wine or strong drink in a twelvemonth
after. A bankrupt shall be *[658] Catademiatus in Amphitheatro*, publicly
shamed, and he that cannot pay his debts, if by riot or negligence he
have been impoverished, shall be for a twelvemonth imprisoned, if in that
space his creditors be not satisfied, *[659]*he shall be hanged. He *[660]*that
commits sacrilege shall lose his hands; he that bears false witness, or is
of perjury convicted, shall have his tongue cut out, except he redeem it
with his head. Murder, *[661]* adultery, shall be punished by
death, *[662]*but not theft, except it be some more grievous offence, or
notorious offenders: otherwise they shall be condemned to the galleys,
mines, be his slaves whom they have offended, during their lives. I hate
all hereditary slaves, and that *duram Persarum legem* as *[663]*Brisonius
calls it; or as *[664]*Ammianus, *impendio formidatas et abominandas leges,
per quas ob noxam unius, omnis propinquitas perit*hard law that wife and
children, friends and allies, should suffer for the father's offence.
No man shall marry until he *[665]*be 25, no woman till she be
20, *[666] nisi alitur dispensatum fuerit*. If one *[667]*die, the other party
shall not marry till six months after; and because many families are
compelled to live niggardly, exhaust and undone by great
dowers, *[668]*none shall be given at all, or very little, and that by
supervisors rated, they that are foul shall have a greater portion; if fair,
none at all, or very little: *[669]*howsoever not to exceed such a rate as
those supervisors shall think fit. And when once they come to those
years, poverty shall hinder no man from marriage, or any other
respect, *[670]*but all shall be rather enforced than hindered, *[671]*except

they be *[672]*dismembered, or grievously deformed, infirm, or visited with some enormous hereditary disease, in body or mind; in such cases upon a great pain, or mulct, *[673]*man or woman shall not marry, other order shall be taken for them to their content. If people overabound, they shall be eased by *[674]*colonies.

*[675]*No man shall wear weapons in any city. The same attire shall be kept, and that proper to several callings, by which they shall be distinguished. *[676]Luxus funerum* shall be taken away, that intempestive expense moderated, and many others. Brokers, takers of pawns, biting usurers, I will not admit; yet because *hic cum hominibus non cum diis agitur*, we converse here with men, not with gods, and for the hardness of men's hearts I will tolerate some kind of usury.*[677]*If we were honest, I confess, *si probi essemus*, we should have no use of it, but being as it is, we must necessarily admit it. Howsoever most divines contradict it, *dicimus inficias, sed vox ea sola reperta est*, it must be winked at by politicians. And yet some great doctors approve of it, Calvin, Bucer, Zanchius, P. Martyr, because by so many grand lawyers, decrees of emperors, princes' statutes, customs of commonwealths, churches' approbations it is permitted, &c. I will therefore allow it. But to no private persons, nor to every man that will, to orphans only, maids, widows, or such as by reason of their age, sex, education, ignorance of trading, know not otherwise how to employ it; and those so approved, not to let it out apart, but to bring their money to a *[678]*common bank which shall be allowed in every city, as in Genoa, Geneva, Nuremberg, Venice, at *[679]*5, 6, 7, not above 8 per centum, as the supervisors, or *aerarii praefecti* shall think fit. *[680]*And as it shall not be lawful for each man to be an usurer that will, so shall it not be lawful for all to take up money at use, not to prodigals and spendthrifts, but to merchants, young tradesmen, such as stand in need, or know honestly how to employ it, whose necessity, cause and condition the said supervisors shall approve of.

I will have no private monopolies, to enrich one man, and beggar a multitude, *[681]*multiplicity of offices, of supplying by deputies, weights and measures, the same throughout, and those rectified by the *Primum mobile* and sun's motion, threescore miles to a degree according to observation, 1000 geometrical paces to a mile, five foot to a pace, twelve inches to a foot, &c. and from measures known it is an easy matter to rectify weights, &c. to cast up all, and resolve bodies by algebra, stereometry. I hate wars if they be not *ad populi salutem* upon urgent occasion, *[682]odimus accipitrim, quia semper vivit in armis [683]* offensive wars, except the cause be very just, I will not allow of. For I do highly magnify that saying of Hannibal to Scipio, in *[684]*Livy, It had been a blessed thing for you and us, if God had given that mind to our predecessors, that you had been content with Italy, we with Africa. For neither Sicily nor Sardinia are worth such cost and pains, so many fleets and armies, or so many famous Captains' lives. *Omnia prius tentanda*, fair means shall first be tried. *[685]Peragit tranquilla potestas, Quod violenta nequit*. I will have them proceed with all moderation: but hear you, Fabius my general, not Minutius, *nam [686]qui Consilio nititur plus hostibus nocet, quam qui sini animi ratione, viribus*: And in such wars to abstain as much as is possible from *[687]*depopulations, burning of towns, massacring of infants, &c. For defensive wars, I will have forces still ready at a small warning, by land and sea, a prepared navy, soldiers *in procinctu, et quam [688]Bonfinius apud Hungaros suos vult, virgam ferream*, and money, which is *nerves belli*, still in a readiness, and a sufficient revenue, a third part as in old *[689]*Rome and Egypt, reserved for the commonwealth; to avoid those heavy taxes and impositions, as well to defray this charge of wars, as also all other public defalcations, expenses, fees, pensions, reparations, chaste sports, feasts, donaries, rewards, and entertainments. All things in this nature especially I will have maturely done, and with great *[690]*deliberation: *ne quid [691]temere, ne quid remisse ac timide fiat; Sid quo feror hospes?* To prosecute the rest would require a volume. *Manum de tabella*, I have been over tedious in this subject; I could have here willingly ranged, but these straits wherein I am included will not permit.

From commonwealths and cities, I will descend to families, which have as many corsives and molestations, as frequent discontents as the rest. Great affinity there is betwixt a political and economical body; they differ only in magnitude and proportion of business (so Scaliger *[692]*writes) as they have both likely the same period, as *[693]*Bodin and *[694]*Peucer hold, out of Plato, six or seven hundred years, so many times they have the same means of their vexation and overthrows; as namely, riot, a common ruin of both, riot in building, riot in profuse spending, riot in apparel, &c. be it in what kind soever, it produceth the same effects. A *[695]*chorographer of ours speaking *obiter* of ancient families, why they are so frequent in the north, continue so long, are so soon extinguished in the south, and so few, gives no other reason but this, *luxus omnia dissipavit*, riot hath consumed all, fine clothes and curious buildings came into this island, as he notes in his annals, not so many years since; *non sine dispendio hospitalitatis* to the decay of hospitality. Howbeit many times that word is mistaken, and under the name of bounty and hospitality, is shrouded riot and prodigality, and that which is commendable in itself well used, hath been mistaken heretofore, is become by his abuse, the bane and utter ruin of many a noble family. For some men live like the rich glutton, consuming themselves and their substance by continual feasting and invitations, with *[696]*Axilon in Homer, keep open house for all comers, giving entertainment to such as visit them, *[697]*keeping a table beyond their means, and a company of idle servants (though not so frequent as of old) are blown up on a sudden; and as Actaeon was by his hounds, devoured by their kinsmen, friends, and multitude of followers. *[698]*It is a wonder that Paulus Jovius relates of our northern countries, what an infinite deal of meat we consume on our tables; that I may truly say, 'tis not bounty, not hospitality, as it is often abused, but riot and excess, gluttony and prodigality; a mere vice; it brings in debt, want, and beggary, hereditary diseases, consumes their fortunes, and overthrows the good temperature of their bodies. To this I might here well add their inordinate expense in building, those fantastical houses, turrets, walks, parks, &c. gaming, excess of pleasure, and that prodigious riot in apparel, by which means they are compelled to break up house, and creep into holes. Sesellius in his commonwealth of *[699]*France, gives three reasons why the French nobility were so frequently bankrupts: First, because they had so many lawsuits and contentions one upon another, which were tedious and costly; by which means it came to pass, that commonly lawyers bought them out of their possessions. A second cause was their riot, they lived beyond their means, and were therefore swallowed up by merchants. (La Nove, a French writer, yields five reasons of his countrymen's poverty, to the same effect almost, and thinks verily if the gentry of France were divided into ten parts, eight of them would be found much impaired, by sales, mortgages, and debts, or wholly sunk in their estates.) The last was immoderate excess in apparel, which consumed their revenues. How this concerns and agrees with our present state, look you. But of this elsewhere. As it is in a man's body, if either head, heart, stomach, liver, spleen, or any one part be misaffected, all the rest suffer with it: so is it with this economical body. If the head be naught, a spendthrift, a drunkard, a whoremaster, a gamester, how shall the family live at ease? *[700]Ipsa si cupiat solus servare, prorsus, non potest hanc familiam*, as Demea said in the comedy, Safety herself cannot save it. A good, honest, painful man many times hath a shrew to his wife, a sickly, dishonest, slothful, foolish, careless woman to his mate, a proud, peevish flirt, a liquorish, prodigal quean, and by that means all goes to ruin: or if they differ in nature, he is thrifty, she spends all, he wise, she sottish and soft; what agreement can there be? what friendship? Like that of the thrush and swallow in Aesop, instead of mutual love, kind compellations, whore and thief is heard, they fling stools at one another's heads. *[701]Quae intemperies vexat hanc familiam?* All enforced marriages commonly produce such effects, or if on their behalves it be well, as to live and agree lovingly together, they may have disobedient and unruly children, that take ill courses to disquiet them, *[702]*their son is a thief, a spendthrift, their daughter a whore; a step *[703]*mother, or a daughter-in-law distempers all; *[704]*or else for want of means, many torturers arise, debts, dues, fees, dowries, jointures, legacies to be paid, annuities issuing out, by means of which, they have not wherewithal to maintain themselves in that pomp as their predecessors have done, bring up or bestow their children to their callings, to their birth and quality, *[705]*and will not descend to their present fortunes. Oftentimes, too, to aggravate the rest, concur many other inconveniences, unthankful friends, decayed friends, bad neighbours, negligent servants *[706]servi furaces, Versipelles, callidi, occlusa sibi mille clavibus reserant, furtimque; raptant, consumunt, liguriunt*; casualties, taxes, mulcts, chargeable offices, vain expenses, entertainments, loss of stock, enmities, emulations, frequent invitations, losses, suretyship, sickness, death of friends, and that which is the gulf of all, improvidence, ill husbandry, disorder and confusion, by which means they are drenched on a sudden in their estates, and at unawares precipitated insensibly into an inextricable labyrinth of debts, cares, woes, want, grief, discontent and melancholy itself.

I have done with families, and will now briefly run over some few sorts and conditions of men. The most secure, happy, jovial, and merry in the world's esteem are princes and great men, free from melancholy: but for

their cares, miseries, suspicions, jealousies, discontents, folly and madness, I refer you to Xenophon's Tyrannus, where king Hieron discourseth at large with Simonides the poet, of this subject. Of all others they are most troubled with perpetual fears, anxieties, insomuch, that as he said in *[707]*Valerius, if thou knewest with what cares and miseries this robe were stuffed, thou wouldst not stoop to take it up. Or put case they be secure and free from fears and discontents, yet they are void *[708]*of reason too oft, and precipitate in their actions, read all our histories, *quos de stultis prodidere stulti*, Iliades, Aeneides, Annales, and what is the subject?
Stultorum regum, et populorum continet aestus.

The giddy tumults and the foolish rage

Of kings and people.

How mad they are, how furious, and upon small occasions, rash and inconsiderate in their proceedings, how they dote, every page almost will witness,

————delirant reges, plectuntur Achivi.

When doting monarchs urge

Unsound resolves, their subjects feel the scourge.

Next in place, next in miseries and discontents, in all manner of hair-brain actions, are great men, *procul a Jove, procul a fulmine*, the nearer the worse. If they live in court, they are up and down, ebb and flow with their princes' favours, *Ingenium vultu statque caditque suo*, now aloft, tomorrow down, as *[709]*Polybius describes them, like so many casting counters, now of gold, tomorrow of silver, that vary in worth as the computant will; now they stand for units, tomorrow for thousands; now before all, and anon behind. Beside, they torment one another with mutual factions, emulations: one is ambitious, another enamoured, a third in debt, a prodigal, overruns his fortunes, a fourth solicitous with cares, gets nothing, &c. But for these men's discontents, anxieties, I refer you to Lucian's Tract, *de mercede conductis*, *[710]*Aeneas Sylvius (*libidinis et stultitiae servos*, he calls them), Agrippa, and many others. Of philosophers and scholars *priscae sapientiae dictatores*, I have already spoken in general terms, those superintendents of wit and learning, men above men, those refined men, minions of the muses,
[711]————mentemque habere queis bonam

Et esse *[712]*corculis datum est.————

*[713]*These acute and subtle sophisters, so much honoured, have as much need of hellebore as others.—*[714]*O medici mediam pertundite venam*. Read Lucian's Piscator, and tell how he esteemed them; Agrippa's

Tract of the vanity of Sciences; nay read their own works, their absurd tenets, prodigious paradoxes, *et risum teneatis amici?* You shall find that of Aristotle true, *nullum magnum ingenium sine mixtura dementiae*, they have a worm as well as others; you shall find a fantastical strain, a fustian, a bombast, a vainglorious humour, an affected style, &c., like a prominent thread in an uneven woven cloth, run parallel throughout their works. And they that teach wisdom, patience, meekness, are the veriest dizzards, harebrains, and most discontent. *[715]*In the multitude of wisdom is grief, and he that increaseth wisdom, increaseth sorrow. I need not quote mine author; they that laugh and contemn others, condemn the world of folly, deserve to be mocked, are as giddy-headed, and lie as open as any other. *[716]*Democritus, that common flouter of folly, was ridiculous himself, barking Menippus, scoffing Lucian, satirical Lucilius, Petronius, Varro, Persius, &c., may be censured with the rest, *Loripedem rectus derideat, Aethiopem albus.* Bale, Erasmus, Hospinian, Vives, Kemnisius, explode as a vast ocean of obs and sols, school divinity. *[717]*A labyrinth of intricable questions, unprofitable contentions, *incredibilem delirationem*, one calls it. If school divinity be so censured, *subtilis [718]Scotus lima veritatis, Occam irrefragabilis, cujus ingenium vetera omnia ingenia subvertit*, &c. Baconthrope, Dr. Resolutus, and *Corculum Theolgiae*, Thomas himself, Doctor *[719]*Seraphicus, *cui dictavit Angelus*, &c. What shall become of humanity? *Ars stulta*, what can she plead? what can her followers say for themselves? Much learning, *[720] cere-diminuit-brum*, hath cracked their sconce, and taken such root, that *tribus Anticyris caput insanabile*, hellebore itself can do no good, nor that renowned *[721]*lantern of Epictetus, by which if any man studied, he should be as wise as he was. But all will not serve; rhetoricians, *in ostentationem loquacitatis multa agitant*, out of their volubility of tongue, will talk much to no purpose, orators can persuade other men what they will, *quo volunt, unde volunt*, move, pacify, &c., but cannot settle their own brains, what saith Tully? *Malo indisertam prudentiam, quam loquacem, stultitiam*; and as *[722]*Seneca seconds him, a wise man's oration should not be polite or solicitous. *[723]*Fabius esteems no better of most of them, either in speech, action, gesture, than as men beside themselves, *insanos declamatores*; so doth Gregory, *Non mihi sapit qui sermone, sed qui factis sapit*. Make the best of him, a good orator is a turncoat, an evil man, *bonus orator pessimus vir*, his tongue is set to sale, he is a mere voice, as *[724]*he said of a nightingale, *dat sine mente sonum*, an hyperbolical liar, a flatterer, a parasite, and as *[725]* Ammianus Marcellinus will, a corrupting cozener, one that doth more mischief by his fair speeches, than he that bribes by money; for a man may with more facility avoid him that circumvents by money, than him that deceives with glozing terms; which made *[726]*Socrates so much abhor and explode them. *[727]*Fracastorius, a famous poet, freely grants all poets to be mad; so doth *[728]*Scaliger; and who doth not? *Aut insanit homo, aut versus facit* (He's mad or making verses), Hor. *Sat. vii. l. 2. Insanire lubet, i. versus componere.* Virg. *3 Ecl.*; so Servius interprets it, all poets are mad, a company of bitter satirists, detractors, or else parasitical applauders: and what is poetry itself, but as Austin holds, *Vinum erroris ab ebriis doctoribus propinatum?* You may give that censure of them in general, which Sir Thomas More once did of Germanus Brixius' poems in particular.

————vehuntur

In rate stultitiae sylvam habitant Furiae.*[729]*

Budaeus, in an epistle of his to Lupsetus, will have civil law to be the tower of wisdom; another honours physic, the quintessence of nature; a third tumbles them both down, and sets up the flag of his own peculiar science. Your supercilious critics, grammatical triflers, note-makers, curious antiquaries, find out all the ruins of wit, *ineptiarum delicias,* amongst the rubbish of old writers; *[730]Pro stultis habent nisi aliquid sufficiant invenire, quod in aliorum scriptis vertant vitio,* all fools with them that cannot find fault; they correct others, and are hot in a cold cause, puzzle themselves to find out how many streets in Rome, houses, gates, towers, Homer's country, Aeneas's mother, Niobe's daughters, *an Sappho publica fuerit? ovum [731]prius extiterit an gallina!* &c. *et alia quae dediscenda essent scire, si scires,* as *[732]*Seneca holds. What clothes the senators did wear in Rome, what shoes, how they sat, where they went to the close-stool, how many dishes in a mess, what sauce, which for the present for an historian to relate, *[733]*according to Lodovic. Vives, is very ridiculous, is to them most precious elaborate stuff, they admired for it, and as proud, as triumphant in the meantime for this discovery, as if they had won a city, or conquered a province; as rich as if they had found a mine of gold ore. *Quosvis auctores absurdis commentis suis percacant et stercorant,* one saith, they bewray and daub a company of books and good authors, with their absurd comments, *correctorum sterquilinia [734]*Scaliger calls them, and show their wit in censuring others, a company of foolish note-makers, humble-bees, dors, or beetles, *inter stercora ut plurimum versantur,* they rake over all those rubbish and dunghills, and prefer a manuscript many times before the Gospel itself, *[735]thesaurum criticum,* before any treasure, and with their deleaturs, *alii legunt sic, meus codex sic habet,* with their *postremae editiones,* annotations, castigations, &c. make books dear, themselves ridiculous, and do nobody good, yet if any man dare oppose or contradict, they are mad, up in arms on a sudden, how many sheets are written in defence, how bitter invectives, what apologies? *[736]Epiphilledes hae sunt ut merae, nugae.* But I dare say no more of, for, with, or against them, because I am liable to their lash as well as others. Of these and the rest of our artists and philosophers, I will generally conclude they are a kind of madmen, as *[737]* Seneca esteems of them, to make doubts and scruples, how to read them truly,

to mend old authors, but will not mend their own lives, or teach us *ingevia sanare, memoriam officiorum ingerere, ac fidem in rebus humanis retinere*, to keep our wits in order, or rectify our manners. *Numquid tibi demens videtur, si istis operam impenderit?* Is not he mad that draws lines with Archimedes, whilst his house is ransacked, and his city besieged, when the whole world is in combustion, or we whilst our souls are in danger, (*mors sequitur, vita fugit*) to spend our time in toys, idle questions, and things of no worth?
That *[738]*lovers are mad, I think no man will deny, *Amare simul et sapere, ipsi Jovi non datur*, Jupiter himself cannot intend both at once. *[739]*Non bene conveniunt, nec in una sede morantur

Majestas et amor.

Tully, when he was invited to a second marriage, replied, he could not *simul amare et sapere* be wise and love both together. *[740]Est orcus ille, vis est immedicabilis, est rabies insana*, love is madness, a hell, an incurable disease; *inpotentem et insanam libidinem [741]*Seneca calls it, an impotent and raging lust. I shall dilate this subject apart; in the meantime let lovers sigh out the rest.
*[742]*Nevisanus the lawyer holds it for an axiom, most women are fools, *[743]consilium foeminis invalidum*; Seneca, men, be they young or old; who doubts it, youth is mad as Elius in Tully, *Stulti adolescentuli*, old age little better, *deleri senes*, &c. Theophrastes, in the 107th year of his age, *[744]*said he then began to be to wise, *tum sapere coepit*, and therefore lamented his departure. If wisdom come so late, where shall we find a wise man? Our old ones dote at threescore-and-ten. I would cite more proofs, and a better author, but for the present, let one fool point at another. *[745]*Nevisanus hath as hard an opinion of *[746]*rich men, wealth and wisdom cannot dwell together, *stultitiam patiuntur opes, [747]*and they do commonly *[748]infatuare cor hominis*, besot men; and as we see it, fools have fortune: *[749]Sapientia non invenitur in terra suaviter viventium.* For beside a natural contempt of learning, which accompanies such kind of men, innate idleness (for they will take no pains), and which *[750]*Aristotle observes, *ubi mens plurima, ibi minima fortuna, ubi plurima fortuna, ibi mens perexigua*, great wealth and little wit go commonly together: they have as much brains some of them in their heads as in their heels; besides this inbred neglect of liberal sciences, and all arts, which should *excolere mentem*, polish the mind, they have most part some gullish humour or other, by which they are led; one is an Epicure, an Atheist, a second a gamester, a third a whoremaster (fit subjects all for a satirist to work upon);
*[751]*Hic nuptarum insanit amoribus, hic puerorum.

One burns to madness for the wedded dame;

Unnatural lusts another's heart inflame.

*[752]*one is mad of hawking, hunting, cocking; another of carousing, horse-riding, spending; a fourth of building, fighting, &c., *Insanit veteres*

statuas Damasippus emendo, Damasippus hath an humour of his own, to be talked of: *[753]*Heliodorus the Carthaginian another. In a word, as Scaliger concludes of them all, they are *Statuae erectae stultitiae,* the very statutes or pillars of folly. Choose out of all stories him that hath been most admired, you shall still find, *multa ad laudem, multa ad vituperationem magnifica,* as *[754]*Berosus of Semiramis; *omnes mortales militia triumphis, divitiis,* &c., *tum et luxu, caede, caeterisque vitiis antecessit,* as she had some good, so had she many bad parts.

Alexander, a worthy man, but furious in his anger, overtaken in drink: Caesar and Scipio valiant and wise, but vainglorious, ambitious: Vespasian a worthy prince, but covetous: *[755]*Hannibal, as he had mighty virtues, so had he many vices; *unam virtutem mille vitia comitantur,* as Machiavel of Cosmo de Medici, he had two distinct persons in him. I will determine of them all, they are like these double or turning pictures; stand before which you see a fair maid, on the one side an ape, on the other an owl; look upon them at the first sight, all is well, but farther examine, you shall find them wise on the one side, and fools on the other; in some few things praiseworthy, in the rest incomparably faulty. I will say nothing of their diseases, emulations, discontents, wants, and such miseries: let poverty plead the rest in Aristophanes' Plutus.
Covetous men, amongst others, are most mad, *[756]*they have all the symptoms of melancholy, fear, sadness, suspicion, &c., as shall be proved in its proper place,
Danda est Hellebori multo pars maxima avaris.

Misers make Anticyra their own;

Its hellebore reserved for them alone.

And yet methinks prodigals are much madder than they, be of what condition they will, that bear a public or private purse; as a *[757]*Dutch writer censured Richard the rich duke of Cornwall, suing to be emperor, for his profuse spending, *qui effudit pecuniam, ante pedes principium Electorum sicut aquam,* that scattered money like water; I do censure them, *Stulta Anglia* (saith he) *quae, tot denariis sponte est privata, stulti principes Alemaniae, qui nobile jus suum pro pecunia vendiderunt;* spendthrifts, bribers, and bribe-takers are fools, and so are *[758]*all they that cannot keep, disburse, or spend their moneys well.
I might say the like of angry, peevish, envious, ambitious; *[759] Anticyras melior sorbere meracas;* Epicures, Atheists, Schismatics, Heretics; *hi omnes habent imaginationem laesam* (saith Nymannus) and their madness shall be evident, 2 Tim. iii. 9. *[760]*Fabatus, an Italian, holds seafaring men all mad; the ship is mad, for it never stands still; the mariners are mad, to expose themselves to such imminent dangers: the waters are raging mad, in perpetual motion: the winds are as mad as the rest, they know not whence they come, whither they would go: and those men are maddest of all that go to sea; for one fool at home, they find forty

abroad. He was a madman that said it, and thou peradventure as mad to read it. *[761]* Felix Platerus is of opinion all alchemists are mad, out of their wits; *[762]*Atheneus saith as much of fiddlers, *et musarum luscinias, [763]* Musicians, *omnes tibicines insaniunt, ubi semel efflant, avolat illico mens*, in comes music at one ear, out goes wit at another. Proud and vainglorious persons are certainly mad; and so are *[764]*lascivious; I can feel their pulses beat hither; horn-mad some of them, to let others lie with their wives, and wink at it. To insist *[765]*in all particulars, were an Herculean task, to *[766]*reckon up *[767]insanas substructiones, insanos labores, insanum luxum*, mad labours, mad books, endeavours, carriages, gross ignorance, ridiculous actions, absurd gestures; *insanam gulam, insaniam villarum, insana jurgia*, as Tully terms them, madness of villages, stupend structures; as those Egyptian Pyramids, Labyrinths and Sphinxes, which a company of crowned asses, *ad ostentationem opum*, vainly built, when neither the architect nor king that made them, or to what use and purpose, are yet known: to insist in their hypocrisy, inconstancy, blindness, rashness, *dementem temeritatem*, fraud, cozenage, malice, anger, impudence, ingratitude, ambition, gross superstition, *[768]tempora infecta et adulatione sordida*, as in Tiberius' times, such base flattery, stupend, parasitical fawning and colloguing, &c. brawls, conflicts, desires, contentions, it would ask an expert Vesalius to anatomise every member. Shall I say? Jupiter himself, Apollo, Mars, &c. doted; and monster-conquering Hercules that subdued the world, and helped others, could not relieve himself in this, but mad he was at last. And where shall a man walk, converse with whom, in what province, city, and not meet with Signior Deliro, or Hercules Furens, Maenads, and Corybantes? Their speeches say no less. *[769]E fungis nati homines*, or else they fetched their pedigree from those that were struck by Samson with the jaw-bone of an ass. Or from Deucalion and Pyrrha's stones, for *durum genus sumus, [770] marmorei sumus*, we are stony-hearted, and savour too much of the stock, as if they had all heard that enchanted horn of Astolpho, that English duke in Ariosto, which never sounded but all his auditors were mad, and for fear ready to make away with themselves; *[771]*or landed in the mad haven in the Euxine sea of *Daphnis insana*, which had a secret quality to dementate; they are a company of giddy-heads, afternoon men, it is Midsummer moon still, and the dog-days last all the year long, they are all mad. Whom shall I then except? Ulricus Huttenus *[772]nemo, nam, nemo omnibus horis sapit, Nemo nascitur sine vitiis, Crimine Nemo caret, Nemo sorte sua vivit contentus, Nemo in amore sapit, Nemo bonus, Nemo sapiens, Nemo, est ex omni parti beatus*, &c. *[773]*and therefore Nicholas Nemo, or Monsieur Nobody shall go free, *Quid valeat nemo, Nemo referre potest*? But whom shall I except in the second place? such as are silent, *vir sapit qui pauca loquitur, [774]*no better way to avoid folly and madness, than by taciturnity. Whom in a third? all senators, magistrates; for all fortunate men are wise, and conquerors valiant, and so are all great men, *non est bonum ludere cum diis*, they are wise by authority, good by their office and place, *his licet impune pessimos esse*, (some say) we must not speak of them, neither is it fit; *per me sint omnia protinus alba*, I will not think

amiss of them. Whom next? Stoics? *Sapiens Stoicus*, and he alone is subject to no perturbations, as *[775]*Plutarch scoffs at him, he is not vexed with torments, or burnt with fire, foiled by his adversary, sold of his enemy: though he be wrinkled, sand-blind, toothless, and deformed; yet he is most beautiful, and like a god, a king in conceit, though not worth a groat. He never dotes, never mad, never sad, drunk, because virtue cannot be taken away, as *[776]*Zeno holds, by reason of strong apprehension, but he was mad to say so. *[777]Anticyrae caelo huic est opus aut dolabra*, he had need to be bored, and so had all his fellows, as wise as they would seem to be. Chrysippus himself liberally grants them to be fools as well as others, at certain times, upon some occasions, *amitti virtutem ait per ebrietatem, aut atribilarium morbum*, it may be lost by drunkenness or melancholy, he may be sometimes crazed as well as the rest: *[778]ad summum sapiens nisi quum pituita molesta*. I should here except some Cynics, Menippus, Diogenes, that Theban Crates; or to descend to these times, that omniscient, only wise fraternity *[779]*of the Rosicrucians, those great theologues, politicians, philosophers, physicians, philologers, artists, &c. of whom S. Bridget, Albas Joacchimus, Leicenbergius, and such divine spirits have prophesied, and made promise to the world, if at least there be any such (Hen. *[780]*Neuhusius makes a doubt of it, *[781]* Valentinus Andreas and others) or an Elias artifex their Theophrastian master; whom though Libavius and many deride and carp at, yet some will have to be the *[782]*renewer of all arts and sciences, reformer of the world, and now living, for so Johannes Montanus Strigoniensis, that great patron of Paracelsus, contends, and certainly avers *[783]*a most divine man, and the quintessence of wisdom wheresoever he is; for he, his fraternity, friends, &c. are all *[784]*betrothed to wisdom, if we may believe their disciples and followers. I must needs except Lipsius and the Pope, and expunge their name out of the catalogue of fools. For besides that parasitical testimony of Dousa,
A Sole exoriente Maeotidas usque paludes,

Nemo est qui justo se aequiparare queat.*[785]*

Lipsius saith of himself, that he was *[786]humani generis quidem paedagogus voce et stylo*, a grand signior, a master, a tutor of us all, and for thirteen years he brags how he sowed wisdom in the Low Countries, as Ammonius the philosopher sometimes did in Alexandria, *[787]cum humanitate literas et sapientiam cum prudentia: antistes sapientiae*, he shall be *Sapientum Octavus*. The Pope is more than a man, as *[788]*his parrots often make him, a demigod, and besides his holiness cannot err, *in Cathedra* belike: and yet some of them have been magicians, Heretics, Atheists, children, and as Platina saith of John 22, *Et si vir literatus, multa stoliditatem et laevitatem prae se ferentia egit, stolidi et socordis vir ingenii*, a scholar sufficient, yet many things he did foolishly, lightly. I can say no more than in particular, but in general terms to the rest, they are all mad, their wits are evaporated, and, as Ariosto feigns, *l.*

34, kept in jars above the moon.

Some lose their wits with love, some with ambition,

Some following *[789]*Lords and men of high condition.

Some in fair jewels rich and costly set,

Others in Poetry their wits forget.

Another thinks to be an Alchemist,

Till all be spent, and that his number's mist.

Convicted fools they are, madmen upon record; and I am afraid past cure many of them, *[790]crepunt inguina*, the symptoms are manifest, they are all of Gotam parish:

*[791]*Quum furor haud dubius, quum sit manifesta phrenesis,

Since madness is indisputable, since frenzy is obvious.

what remains then *[792]*but to send for Lorarios, those officers to carry them all together for company to Bedlam, and set Rabelais to be their physician.

If any man shall ask in the meantime, who I am that so boldly censure others, *tu nullane habes vitia*? have I no faults? *[793]*Yes, more than thou hast, whatsoever thou art. *Nos numerus sumus*, I confess it again, I am as foolish, as mad as any one.
*[794]*Insanus vobis videor, non deprecor ipse,

Quo minus insanus,——

I do not deny it, *demens de populo dematur*. My comfort is, I have more fellows, and those of excellent note. And though I be not so right or so discreet as I should be, yet not so mad, so bad neither, as thou perhaps takest me to be.
To conclude, this being granted, that all the world is melancholy, or mad, dotes, and every member of it, I have ended my task, and sufficiently illustrated that which I took upon me to demonstrate at first. At this present I have no more to say; *His sanam mentem Democritus*, I can but wish myself and them a good physician, and all of us a better mind. And although for the above-named reasons, I had a just cause to undertake this subject, to point at these particular species of dotage, that so men might acknowledge their imperfections, and seek to reform what is amiss; yet I have a more serious intent at this time; and to omit all impertinent digressions, to say no more of such as are improperly melancholy, or metaphorically mad, lightly mad, or in disposition, as

stupid, angry, drunken, silly, sottish, sullen, proud, vainglorious, ridiculous, beastly, peevish, obstinate, impudent, extravagant, dry, doting, dull, desperate, harebrain, &c. mad, frantic, foolish, heteroclites, which no new *[795]* hospital can hold, no physic help; my purpose and endeavour is, in the following discourse to anatomise this humour of melancholy, through all its parts and species, as it is an habit, or an ordinary disease, and that philosophically, medicinally, to show the causes, symptoms, and several cures of it, that it may be the better avoided. Moved thereunto for the generality of it, and to do good, it being a disease so frequent, as *[796]* Mercurialis observes, in these our days; so often happening, saith *[797]*Laurentius, in our miserable times, as few there are that feel not the smart of it. Of the same mind is Aelian Montaltus, *[798]*Melancthon, and others; *[799]*Julius Caesar Claudinus calls it the fountain of all other diseases, and so common in this crazed age of ours, that scarce one of a thousand is free from it; and that splenetic hypochondriacal wind especially, which proceeds from the spleen and short ribs. Being then a disease so grievous, so common, I know not wherein to do a more general service, and spend my time better, than to prescribe means how to prevent and cure so universal a malady, an epidemical disease, that so often, so much crucifies the body and mind.

If I have overshot myself in this which hath been hitherto said, or that it is, which I am sure some will object, too fantastical, too light and comical for a Divine, too satirical for one of my profession, I will presume to answer with *[800]*Erasmus, in like case, 'tis not I, but Democritus, Democritus *dixit*: you must consider what it is to speak in one's own or another's person, an assumed habit and name; a difference betwixt him that affects or acts a prince's, a philosopher's, a magistrate's, a fool's part, and him that is so indeed; and what liberty those old satirists have had; it is a cento collected from others; not I, but they that say it. *[801]*Dixero si quid forte jocosius, hoc mihi juris

Cum venia, dabis——

Yet some indulgence I may justly claim,

If too familiar with another's fame.

Take heed you mistake me not. If I do a little forget myself, I hope you will pardon it. And to say truth, why should any man be offended, or take exceptions at it?
Licuit, semperque licebit,

Parcere personis, dicere de vitiis.

It lawful was of old, and still will be,

To speak of vice, but let the name go free.

I hate their vices, not their persons. If any be displeased, or take aught unto himself, let him not expostulate or cavil with him that said it (so did *[802]*Erasmus excuse himself to Dorpius, *si parva licet componere magnis*) and so do I; but let him be angry with himself, that so betrayed and opened his own faults in applying it to himself: *[803]*if he be guilty and deserve it, let him amend, whoever he is, and not be angry. He that hateth correction is a fool, Prov. xii. 1. If he be not guilty, it concerns him not; it is not my freeness of speech, but a guilty conscience, a galled back of his own that makes him wince.

Suspicione si quis errabit sua,

Et rapiet ad se, quod erit commune omnium,

Stulte nudabit animi conscientiam.*[804]*

I deny not this which I have said savours a little of Democritus; *[805] Quamvis ridentem dicere verum quid velat*; one may speak in jest, and yet speak truth. It is somewhat tart, I grant it; *acriora orexim excitant embammata*, as he said, sharp sauces increase appetite, *[806]nec cibus ipse juvat morsu fraudatus aceti*. Object then and cavil what thou wilt, I ward all with *[807]*Democritus's buckler, his medicine shall salve it; strike where thou wilt, and when: *Democritus dixit*, Democritus will answer it. It was written by an idle fellow, at idle times, about our Saturnalian or Dionysian feasts, when as he said, *nullum libertati periculum est*, servants in old Rome had liberty to say and do what them list. When our countrymen sacrificed to their goddess *[808]*Vacuna, and sat tippling by their Vacunal fires. I writ this, and published this οὖτις ἔλεγεν, it is *neminis nihil*. The time, place, persons, and all circumstances apologise for me, and why may not I then be idle with others? speak my mind freely? If you deny me this liberty, upon these presumptions I will take it: I say again, I will take it.

*[809]*Si quis est qui dictum in se inclementius

Existimavit esse, sic existimet.

If any man take exceptions, let him turn the buckle of his girdle, I care not. I owe thee nothing (Reader), I look for no favour at thy hands, I am independent, I fear not.

No, I recant, I will not, I care, I fear, I confess my fault, acknowledge a great offence,
————motos praestat componere fluctus.

————let's first assuage the troubled waves

I have overshot myself, I have spoken foolishly, rashly, unadvisedly, absurdly, I have anatomised mine own folly. And now methinks upon a sudden I am awaked as it were out of a dream; I have had a raving fit, a fantastical fit, ranged up and down, in and out, I have insulted over the most kind of men, abused some, offended others, wronged myself; and now being recovered, and perceiving mine error, cry with *[810]*Orlando, *Solvite me*, pardon (*o boni*) that which is past, and I will make you amends in that which is to come; I promise you a more sober discourse in my following treatise.

If through weakness, folly, passion, *[811]*discontent, ignorance, I have said amiss, let it be forgotten and forgiven. I acknowledge that of *[812]* Tacitus to be true, *Asperae facetiae, ubi nimis ex vero traxere, acrem sui memoriam relinquunt*, a bitter jest leaves a sting behind it: and as an honourable man observes, *[813]*They fear a satirist's wit, he their memories. I may justly suspect the worst; and though I hope I have wronged no man, yet in Medea's words I will crave pardon,
———Illud jam voce extrema peto,

Ne si qua noster dubius effudit dolor,

Maneant in animo verba, sed melior tibi

Memoria nostri subeat, haec irae data

Obliterentur———

And in my last words this I do desire,

That what in passion I have said, or ire,

May be forgotten, and a better mind,

Be had of us, hereafter as you find.

I earnestly request every private man, as Scaliger did Cardan, not to take offence. I will conclude in his lines, *Si me cognitum haberes, non solum donares nobis has facetias nostras, sed etiam indignum duceres, tam humanum aninum, lene ingenium, vel minimam suspicionem deprecari oportere*. If thou knewest my *[814]*modesty and simplicity, thou wouldst easily pardon and forgive what is here amiss, or by thee misconceived. If hereafter anatomizing this surly humour, my hand slip, as an unskilful 'prentice I lance too deep, and cut through skin and all at unawares, make it smart, or cut awry, *[815]*pardon a rude hand, an unskilful knife, 'tis a most difficult thing to keep an even tone, a perpetual tenor, and not sometimes to lash out; *difficile est Satyram non scribere*, there be so many objects to divert, inward perturbations to molest, and the very best

may sometimes err; *aliquando bonus dormitat Homerus* (some times that
excellent Homer takes a nap), it is impossible not in so much to
overshoot;—*opere in longo fas est obrepere, summum.* But what needs all
this? I hope there will no such cause of offence be given; if there
be, *[816]Nemo aliquid recognoscat, nos mentimur omnia.* I'll deny all (my
last refuge), recant all, renounce all I have said, if any man except, and
with as much facility excuse, as he can accuse; but I presume of thy
good favour, and gracious acceptance (gentle reader). Out of an assured
hope and confidence thereof, I will begin.

LECTORI MALE FERIATO.
Tu vero cavesis edico quisquis es, ne temere sugilles Auctorem hujusce
operis, aut cavillator irrideas. Imo ne vel ex aliorum censura tacite
obloquaris (vis dicam verbo) nequid nasutulus inepte improbes, aut falso
fingas. Nam si talis revera sit, qualem prae se fert Junior Democritus,
seniori Democrito saltem affinis, aut ejus Genium vel tantillum sapiat;
actum de te, censorem aeque ac delatorem *[817]*aget econtra (*petulanti
splene cum sit*) sufflabit te in jocos, comminuet in sales, addo etiam, *et
deo risui* te sacrificabit.
Iterum moneo, ne quid cavillere, ne dum Democritum Juniorem conviciis
infames, aut ignominiose vituperes, de te non male sentientem, tu idem
audias ab amico cordato, quod olim vulgus Abderitanum
ab *[818]* Hippocrate, concivem bene meritum et popularem suum
Democritum, pro insano habens. *Ne tu Democrite sapis, stulti autem et
insani Abderitae.*
*[819]*Abderitanae pectora plebis habes.

Haec te paucis admonitum volo (male feriate Lector) abi.

TO THE READER AT LEISURE.
Whoever you may be, I caution you against rashly defaming the author of
this work, or cavilling in jest against him. Nay, do not silently reproach
him in consequence of others' censure, nor employ your wit in foolish
disapproval, or false accusation. For, should Democritus Junior prove to
be what he professes, even a kinsman of his elder namesake, or be ever
so little of the same kidney, it is all over with you: he will become both
accuser and judge of you in your spleen, will dissipate you in jests,
pulverise you into salt, and sacrifice you, I can promise you, to the God
of Mirth.
I further advise you, not to asperse, or calumniate, or slander,
Democritus Junior, who possibly does not think ill of you, lest you may
hear from some discreet friend, the same remark the people of Abdera
did from Hippocrates, of their meritorious and popular fellow-citizen,
whom they had looked on as a madman; It is not that you, Democritus,
that art wise, but that the people of Abdera are fools and madmen. You
have yourself an Abderitian soul; and having just given you, gentle
reader, these few words of admonition, farewell.
Heraclite fleas, misero sic convenit aevo,

Nil nisi turpe vides, nil nisi triste vides.

Ride etiam, quantumque lubet, Democrite ride

Non nisi vana vides, non nisi stulta vides.

Is fletu, his risu modo gaudeat, unus utrique

Sit licet usque labor, sit licet usque dolor.

Nunc opes est (nam totus eheu jam desipit orbis)

Mille Heraclitis, milleque Democritis.

Nunc opus est (tanta est insania) transeat omnis

Mundus in Anticyras, gramen in Helleborum.

Weep, O Heraclitus, it suits the age,

Unless you see nothing base, nothing sad.

Laugh, O Democritus, as much as you please,

Unless you see nothing either vain or foolish.

Let one rejoice in smiles, the other in tears;

Let the same labour or pain be the office of both.

Now (for alas! how foolish the world has become),

A thousand Heraclitus', a thousand Democritus' are required.

Now (so much does madness prevail), all the world must be

Sent to Anticyra, to graze on Hellebore.

Preface | *Part 1* | *Part 2* | *Part 3*

Notes

1. His elder brother was William Burton, the Leicestershire antiquary, born 24th August, 1575, educated at Sutton Coldfield, admitted commoner, or gentleman commoner, of Brazen Nose College, 1591; at the Inner Temple, 20th May, 1593; B. A. 22d June, 1594; and afterwards a barrister and reporter in the Court of Common Pleas. But his natural

genius, says Wood, leading him to the studies of heraldry, genealogies, and antiquities, he became excellent in those obscure and intricate matters; and look upon him as a gentleman, was accounted, by all that knew him, to be the best of his time for those studies, as may appear by his 'Description of Leicestershire.' His weak constitution not permitting him to follow business, he retired into the country, and his greatest work, The Description of Leicestershire, was published in folio, 1623. He died at Falde, after suffering much in the civil war, 6th April, 1645, and was buried in the parish church belonging thereto, called Hanbury.

2. This is Wood's account. His will says, Nuneaton; but a passage in this work [see fol. 304,] mentions Sutton Coldfield; probably he may have been at both schools.

3. So in the Register.

4. So in the Register.

5. Originating, perhaps, in a note, p. 448, 6th edit. (p. 455 of the present), in which a book is quoted as having been printed at Paris 1624, *seven* years after Burton's first edition. As, however, the editions after that of 1621, are regularly marked in succession to the eighth, printed in 1676, there seems very little reason to doubt that, in the note above alluded to, either 1624 has been a misprint for 1628, or *seven* years for *three* years. The numerous typographical errata in other parts of the work strongly aid this latter supposition.

6. Haec comice dicta cave ne male capias.

7. Seneca in ludo in mortem Claudii Caesaris.

8. Lib. de Curiositate.

9. Modo haec tibi usui sint, quemvis auctorem fingito. Wecker.

10. Lib. 10, c. 12. Multa a male feriatis in Democriti nomine commenta data, nobilitatis, auctoritatisque ejus perfugio utentibus.

11. Martialis. lib. 10, epigr. 14.

12. Juv. sat. 1.

13. Auth. Pet. Besseo edit. Coloniae, 1616.

14. Hip. Epist. Dameget.

15. Laert. lib 9.

16. Hortulo sibi cellulam seligens, ibique seipsum includens, vixit solitarius.

17. Floruit Olympiade 80; 700 annis post Troiam.

18. Diacos. quod cunctis operibus facile excellit. Laert.

19. Col. lib. 1. c. 1.

20. Const. lib. de agric. passim.

21. Volucrum voces et linguas intelligere se dicit Abderitans Ep. Hip.

22. Sabellicus exempl., lib. 10. Oculis se privavit, ut melius contemplationi operam daret, sublimi vir ingenio, profundae cogitationis, &c.

23. Naturalia, moralia, mathematica, liberales disciplinas, artiumque omnium peritiam callebat.

24. Nothing in nature's power to contrive of which he has not written.

25. Veni Athenas, et nemo me novit.

26. Idem contemptui et admirationi habitus.

27. Solebat ad portam ambulare, et inde, &c. Hip. Ep. Dameg.

28. Perpetuorisu pulmonem agitare solebat Democritus. Juv. Sat. 7.

29. Non sum dignus praestare matella. Mart.

30. Christ Church in Oxford.

31. Praefat. Hist.

32. Keeper of our college library, lately revived by Otho Nicolson, Esquire.

33. Scaliger.

34. Somebody in everything, nobody in each thing.

35. In Theat.

36. Phil. Stoic. li. diff. 8. Dogma cupidis et curiosis ingeniis imprimendum, ut sit talis qui nulli rei serviat, aut exacte unum aliquid

elaboret, alia negligens, ut artifices, &c.

37. Delibare gratum de quocunque cibo, et pittisare de quocunque dolio jucundum.

38. Essays, lib. 3.

39. He that is everywhere is nowhere.

40. Praefat. bibliothec.

41. Ambo fortes et fortunati, Mars idem magisterii dominus juxta primam Leovitii regulam.

42. Hensius.

43. Calide ambientes, solicite litigantes, aut misere excidentes, voces, strepitum contentiones, &c.

44. Cyp. ad Donat. Unice securus, ne excidam in foro, aut in mari Indico bonis eluam, de dote filiae, patrimonio filii non sum solicitus.

45. Not so sagacious an observer as simple a narrator.

46. Hor. Ep. lib. 1. xix., 20.

47. Per. A laughter with a petulant spleen.

48. Hor. lib. 1, sat. 9.

49. Secundum moenia locus erat frondosis populis opacus, vitibusque sponte natis, tenuis prope aqua defluebat, placide murmurans, ubi sedile et domus Democriti conspiciebatur.

50. Ipse composite considebat, super genua volumen habens, et utrinque alia patentia parata, dissectaque animalia cumulatim strata, quorum viscera rimabatur.

51. Cum mundus extra se sit, et mente captus sit, et nesciat se languere, ut medelam adhibeat.

52. Scaliger, Ep. ad Patisonem. Nihil magis lectorem invitat quam in opinatum argilinentum, neque vendibilior merx est quam petulans liber.

53. Lib. xx. c. 11. Miras sequuntur inscriptionum festivitates.

54. Praefat. Nat. Hist. Patri obstetricem parturienti filiae accersenti

moram injicere possunt.

55. Anatomy of Popery, Anatomy of immortality, Angelus salas, Anatomy of Antimony, &c.

56. Cont. l. 4, c. 9. Non est cura melior quam labor.

57. Hor. De Arte Poet.

58. Non quod de novo quid addere, aut a veteribus praetermissum, sed propriae exercitationis causa.

59. Qui novit, neque id quod sentit exprimit, perinde est ac si nesciret.

60. Jovius Praef. Hist.

61. Erasmus.

62. Otium otio dolorem dolore sum solatus.

63. Observat. l. 1.

64. M. Joh. Rous, our Protobib. Oxon. M. Hopper, M. Guthridge, &c.

65. Quae illi audire et legere solent, eorum partim vidi egomet, alia gessi, quae illi literis, ego militando didici, nunc vos existimate facta an dicta pluris sint.

66. Dido Virg. Taught by that Power that pities me, I learn to pity them.

67. Camden, Ipsa elephantiasi correpta elephantiasis hospicium construxit.

68. Iliada post Homerum.

69. Nihil praetermissum quod a quovis dici possit.

70. Martialis.

71. Magis impium mortuorum lucubrationes, quam vestes furari.

72. Eccl. ult.

73. Libros Eunuchi gignunt, steriles pariunt.

74. D. King praefat. lect. Jonas, the late right reverend Lord B. of London.

75. Homines famelici gloriae ad ostentationem eruditionis undique congerunt. Buchananus.

76. Effacinati etiam laudis amore, &c. Justus Baronius.

77. Ex ruinis alienae existimationis sibi gradum ad famam struunt.

78. Exercit. 288.

79. Omnes sibi famam quaerunt et quovis modo in orbem spargi contendunt, ut novae alicujus rei habeantur auctores. Praef. biblioth.

80. Praefat. hist.

81. Plautus.

82. E Democriti puteo.

83. Non tam refertae bibliothecae quam cloacae.

84. Et quicquid cartis amicitur ineptis.

85. Epist. ad Petas. in regno Franciae omnibus scribendi datur libertas, paucis facultas.

86. Olim literae ob homines in precio, nunc sordent ob homines.

87. Ans. pac.

88. Inter tot mille volumina vix unus a cujus lectione quis melior evadat, immo potius non pejor.

89. Palingenius. What does any one, who reads such works, learn or know but dreams and trifling things.

90. Lib. 5. de Sap.

91. Sterile oportet esse ingenium quod in hoc scripturientum pruritus, &c.

92. Cardan, praef. ad Consol.

93. Hor. lib. 1, sat. 4.

94. Epist. lib. 1. Magnum poetarum proventum annus hic attulit, mense Aprili nullus fere dies quo non aliquis recitavit.

95. Idem.

96. Principibus et doctoribus deliberandum relinquo, ut arguantur auctorum furta et milies repetita tollantur, et temere scribendi libido coerceatur, aliter in infinitum progressura.

97. Onerabuntur ingenia, nemo legendis sufficit.

98. Libris obraimur, oculi legendo, manus volitando dolent. Fam. Strada Momo. Lucretius.

99. Quicquid ubique bene dictum facio meum, et illud nunc meis ad compendium, nunc ad fidem et auctoritatem alienis exprimo verbis, omnes auctores meos clientes esse arbitror, &c. Sarisburiensis ad Polycrat. prol.

100. In Epitaph. Nep. illud Cyp. hoc Lact. illud Hilar. est, ita Victorinus, in hunc modum loquutus est Arnobius, &c.

101. Praef. ad Syntax. med.

102. Until a later age and a happier lot produce something more truly grand.

103. In Luc. 10. tom. 2. Pigmei Gigantum humeris impositi plusquam ipsi Gigantes vident.

104. Nec aranearum textus ideo melior quia ex se fila gignuntur, nec noster ideo vilior, quia ex alienis libamus ut apes. Lipsius adversus dialogist.

105. Uno absurdo dato mille sequuntur.

106. Non dubito multos lectores hic fore stultos.

107. Martial, 13, 2.

108. Ut venatores feram e vestigio impresso, virum scriptiuncula. Lips.

109. Hor.

110. Hor.

111. Antwerp. fol. 1607.

112. Muretus.

113. Lipsius.

114. Hor.

115. Fieri non potest, ut quod quisque cogitat, dicat unus. Muretus.

116. Lib. 1. de ord., cap. 11.

117. Erasmus.

118. Annal. Tom. 3. ad annum 360. Est porcus ille qui sacerdotem ex amplitudine redituum sordide demeritur.

119. Erasm. dial.

120. Epist. lib. 6. Cujusque ingenium non statim emergit, nisi materiae fautor, occasio, commendatorque contingat.

121. Praef. hist.

122. Laudari a laudato laus est.

123. Vit. Persii.

124. Minuit praesentia famam.

125. Lipsius Judic. de Seneca.

126. Lib. 10. Plurirmum studii, multam rerum cognitionem, omnem studiorum materiam, &c. multa in eo probanda, multa admiranda.

127. Suet. Arena sine calce.

128. Introduct. ad Sen.

129. Judic. de Sen. Vix aliquis tam absolutus, ut alteri per omnia satisfaciat, nisi longa temporis praescripto, semota judicandi libertate, religione quidam animos occuparis.

130. Hor. Ep. 1, lib. 19.

131. Aeque turpe frigide laudari ac insectanter vituperari. Phavorinus A. Gel. lib. 19, cap. 2.

132. Ovid, trist. 11. eleg 6.

133. Juven. sat. 5.

134. Aut artis inscii aut quaestui magis quam literis student. hab. Cantab. et Lond. Excus. 1976.

135. Ovid. de pont. Eleg. l. 6.

136. Hor.

137. Tom. 3. Philopseud. accepto pessulo, quum carmen quoddam dixisset, effecit ut ambularet, aquam hauriret, urnam pararet, &c.

138. Eusebius, eccles. hist. lib. 6.

139. Stans pede in uno, as he made verses.

140. Virg.

141. Non eadem a summo expectes, minimoque poeta.

142. Stylus hic nullus, praeter parrhesiam.

143. Qui rebus se exercet, verba negligit, et qui callet artem dicendi, nullam disciplinam habet recognitam.

144. Palingenius. Words may be resplendent with ornament, but they contain no marrow within.

145. Cujuscunque orationem vides politam et sollicitam, scito animum in pusilis occupatum, in scriptis nil solidum. Epist. lib. 1. 21.

146. Philostratus, lib. 8. vit. Apol. Negligebat oratoriam facultatem, et penitus aspernabatur ejus professores, quod linguam duntaxat, non autem mentem redderent eruditiorem.

147. Hic enim, quod Seneca de Ponto, bos herbam, ciconia larisam, canis leporem, virgo florem legat.

148. Pet. Nannius not. in Hor.

149. Non hic colonus domicilium habeo, sed topiarii in morem, hinc inde florem vellico, ut canis Nilum lambens.

150. Supra bis mille notabiles errores Laurentii demonstravi, &c.

151. Philo de Con.

152. Virg.

153. Frambesarius, Sennertus, Ferandus, &c.

154. Ter. Adelph.

155. Heaut. Act 1. scen. 1.

156. Gellius. lib. 18, cap. 3.

157. Et inde catena quaedam fit, quae haeredes etiam ligat. Cardan. Hensius.

158. Malle se bellum cum magno principe gerere, quam cum uno ex fratrum mendicantium ordine.

159. Hor. epod. lib. od. 7.

160. Epist. 86, ad Casulam presb.

161. Lib. 12, cap. 1. Mutos nasci, et omni scientia egere satius fuisset, quam sic in propriam perniciem insanire.

162. But it would be better not to write, for silence is the safer course.

163. Infelix mortalitas inutilibus quaestionibus ac disceptationibus vitam traducimus, naturae principes thesauros, in quibus gravissimae morborum medicinae collocatae sunt, interim intactos relinquimus. Nec ipsi solum relinquimus, sed et allos prohibemus, impedimus, condemnamus, ludibriisque afficimus.

164. Quod in praxi minime fortunatus esset, medicinam reliquit, et ordinibus initiatus in Theologia postmodum scripsit. Gesner Bibliotheca.

165. P. Jovius.

166. M. W. Burton, preface to his description of Leicestershire, printed at London by W. Jaggard, for J. White, 1622.

167. In Hygiasticon, neque enim haec tractatio aliena videri debet a theologo, &c. agitur de morbo animae.

168. D. Clayton in comitiis, anno 1621.

169. Hor.

170. Lib. de pestil.

171. In Newark in Nottinghamshire. Cum duo edificasset castella, ad tollendam structionis invidiam, et expiandam maculam, duo instituit caenobia, et collegis relgiosis implevit.

172. Ferdinando de Quir. anno 1612. Amsterdami impress.

173. Praefat. ad Characteres: Spero enim (O Policles) libros nostros meliores inde futuros, quod istiusmodi memoriae mandata reliquerimus, ex preceptis et exemplis nostris ad vitam accommodatis, ut se inde corrigant.

174. Part 1. sect. 3.

175. praef. lectori.

176. Ep. 2. 1. 2. ad Donatum. Paulisper te crede subduci in ardui montis verticem celsiorem, speculare inde rerum jacentium facies, et oculis in diversa porrectis, fluctuantis mundi turbines intuere, jam simul aut ridebis aut misereberis, &c.

177. Controv. l. 2. cont. 7. et l. 6. cont.

178. Horatius.

179. Idem, Hor. l. 2. Satyra 3. Damasipus Stoicus probat omnes stultos insanire.

180. Tom. 2. sympos. lib. 5. c. 6. Animi affectiones, si diutius inhaereant, pravos generant habitus.

181. Lib. 28, cap. 1. Synt. art. mir. Morbus nihil est aliud quam dissolutio quaedam ac perturbatio foederis in corpore existentis, sicut et sanitas est consentientis bene corporis consummatio quaedam.

182. Lib. 9. Geogr. Plures olim gentes navigabant illuc sanitatis causa.

183. Eccles. i. 24.

184. Jure haereditario sapere jubentur. Euphormio Satyr.

185. Apud quos virtus, insania et furor esse dicitur.

186. Calcagninus Apol. omnes mirabantur, putantes illisam iri stultitiam. Sed praeter expectationem res evenit, Audax stultitia in eam irruit, &c. illa cedit irrisa, et plures hinc habet sectatores stultitia.

187. Non est respondendum stulto secundum stultitiam.

188. 2 Reg. 7.

189. Lib. 10. ep. 97.

190. Aug. ep. 178.

191. Quis nisi mentis inops, &c.

192. Quid insanius quam pro momentanea felicitate aeternis te mancipare suppliciis?

193. In fine Phaedonis. Hic finis fuit amici nostri o Eucrates, nostro quidem judicio omnium quos experti sumus optimi et apprime sapientissimi, et justissimi.

194. Xenop. l. 4. de dictis Socratis ad finem, talis fuit Socrates quem omnium optimum et felicissimum statuam.

195. Lib. 25. Platonis Convivio.

196. Lucretius.

197. Anaxagoras olim mens dictus ab antiquis.

198. Regula naturae, naturae miraculum, ipsa eruditio daemonium hominis, sol scientiarum, mare, sophia, antistes literarum et sapientiae, ut Scioppius olim de Scal, et Heinsius. Aquila In nubibus Imperator literatorum, columen literarum, abyssus eruditionis, ocellus Europae, Scaliger.

199. Lib. 3. de sap c. 17. et 20. omnes Philosophi, aut stulti, aut insani; nulla anus nullus aeger ineptius deliravit.

200. Democritus a Leucippo doctus, haeridatem stultitiae reliquit Epic.

201. Hor. car. lib. 1. od. 34. 1. epicur.

202. Nihil interest inter hos et bestias nisi quod loquantur. de sa. l. 26. c. 8.

203. Cap. de virt.

204. Neb. et Ranis.

205. Omnium disciplinarum ignarus.

206. Omnium disciplinarum ignarus.

207. Pulchrorum adolescentum causa frequentur gymnasium, obibat, &c.

208. Seneca. Seis rotunda metiri, sed non tuum animum.

209. Ab uberibus sapientia lactati caecutire non possunt.

210. Cor Xenodoti et jecur Cratetis.

211. Lib. de nat. boni.

212. Hic profundissimae Sophiae fodinae.

213. Panegyr. Trajano omnes actiones exprobrare stultitiam videntur.

214. Ser. 4. in domi Pal. Mundus qui ob antiquitatem deberet esse sapiens, semper stultizat, et nullis flagellis alteratur, sed ut puer vult rosis et floribus coronari.

215. Insanum te omnes pueri, clamantque puellae. Hor.

216. Plautus Aubular.

217. Adelph. act. 5. scen. 8.

218. Tully Tusc. 5. fortune, not wisdom, governs our lives.

219. Plato Apologia Socratis.

220. Ant. Dial.

221. Lib. 3. de sap. pauci ut video sanae mentis sunt.

222. Stulte et incaute omnia agi video.

223. Insania non omnibus eadem, Erasm. chil. 3. cent. 10. nemo mortalium qui non aliqua in re desipit, licet alius alio morbo laboret, hic libidinis, ille avaritiae, ambitionis, invidiae.

224. Hor. l. 2. sat. 3.

225. Lib. 1. de aulico. Est in unoquoque nostrum seminarium aliquod stultitiae, quod si quando excitetur, in infinitum facile excrescit.

226. Primaque lux vitae prima juroris erat.

227. Tibullus, stulti praetereunt dies, their wits are a wool-gathering. So fools commonly dote.

228. Dial. contemplantes, Tom: 2.

229. Catullus.

230. Sub ramosa platano sedentem, solum, discalceatum, super lapidem, valde pallidum ac macilentum, promissa barba, librum super genibus habentem.

231. De furore, mania melancholia scribo, ut sciam quo pacto in hominibus gignatur, fiat, crescat, cumuletur, minuatur; haec inquit animalia quae vides propterea seco, non Dei opera perosus, sed fellis bilisque naturam disquirens.

232. Aust. l. 1. in Gen. Jumenti & servi tui obsequium rigide postulas, et tu nullum praestas aliis, nec ipsi Deo.

233. Uxores ducunt, mox foras ejiciunt.

234. Pueros amant, mox fastidiunt.

235. Quid hoc ab insania deest?

236. Reges eligunt, deponunt.

237. Contra parentes, fratres, cives, perpetuo rixantur, et inimicitias agunt.

238. Idola inanimata amant, animata odio habent, sic pontificii.

239. Credo equidem vivos ducent e marmore vultus.

240. Suam stultitiam perspicit nemo, sed alter alterum deridet.

241. Denique sit finis querendi, cumque habeas plus, pauperiem metuas minis, et finire laborem incipias, partis quod avebas, utere Hor.

242. Astutam vapido servat sub pectore vulpem. Et cum vulpo positus pariter vulpinarier. Cretizan dum cum Crete.

243. Qui fit Mecaenas ut nemo quam sibi sortem. Seu ratio dederit, seu sors objecerit, illa contentus vivat, &c. Hor.

244. Diruit, aedificat, mutat quadrata rotundis. Trajanus pontem struxit super Danubium, quem successor ejus Adrianus statim demolitus.

245. Qua quid in re ab infantibus differunt, quibus mens et sensus sine ratione inest, quicquid sese his offert volupe est.

246. Idem Plut.

247. Ut insaniae causam disquiram bruta macto et seco, cum hoc potius

in hominibus investigandum esset.

248. Totus a nativitate morbus est.

249. In vigore furibundus, quum decrescit insanabilis.

250. Cyprian. ad Donatum. Qui sedet crimina judicaturus, &c.

251. Tu pessimus omnium latro es, as a thief told Alexander in Curtius. Damnat foras judex, quod intus operatur, Cyprian.

252. Vultus magna cura, magna animi incuria. Am. Marcel.

253. Horrenda res est, vix duo verba sine mendacio proferuntur: et quamvis solenniter homines ad veritatem dicendum invitentur, pejerare tamen non dubitant, ut ex decem testibus vix unus verum dicat. Calv. in 8 John, Serm 1.

254. Sapientiam insaniam esse dicunt.

255. Siquidem sapientiae suae admiratione me complevit, offendi sapientissimum virum, qui salvos potest omnes homines reddere.

256. E. Graec. epig.

257. Plures Democriti nunc non sufficiunt, opus Democrito qui Democritum rideat. Eras Moria.

258. Polycrat. lib. 3. cap. 8. e Petron.

259. Ubi omnes delirabant, omnes insani, &c. hodie nauta, cras philosophus; hodie faber, cras pharmacopola; hic modo regem agebat multo sattellitio, tiara, et sceptro ornatus, nunc vili amictus centiculo, asinum elitellarium impellit.

260. Calcagninus Apol. Crysalus e caeteris auro dives, manicato pepio et tiara conspicuus, levis alioquin et nullius consilii, &c. magno fastu ingredienti assurgunt dii, &c.

261. Sed hominis levitatem Jupiter perspiciens, at tu (iniquit) esto bombilio, &c. protinusque vestis illa manicata in alas versa est, et mortales inde Chrysalides vocant hujusmodi homines.

262. You will meet covetous fools and prodigal sycophants everywhere.

263. Juven.

264. Juven.

265. De bello Jud. l. 8. c. 11. Iniquitates vestrae neminem latent, inque dies singulos certamen habetis quis pejor sit.

266. Hor.

267. Lib. 5. Epist. 8.

268. Hor.

269. Superstitio est insanus error.

270. Lib. 8. hist. Belg.

271. Lucan.

272. Father Angelo, the Duke of Joyeux, going barefoot over the Alps to Rome, &c.

273. Si cui intueri vacet quae patiuntur superstitiosi, invenies tam indecora honestis, tam indigna liberis, tam dissimilia sanis, ut nemo fuerit dubitaturus furere eos, si cum paucioribus fuerent. Senec.

274. Quid dicam de eorum indulgentiis, oblationibus, votis, solutionibus, jejuniis, coenobiis, somniis, horis, organis, cantilenis, campanis, simulachris, missis, purgatoriis, mitris, breviariis, bullis, lustralibus, aquis, rasuris, unctionibus, candelis, calicibus, crucibus, mappis, cereis, thuribulis, incantationibus, exorcismis, sputis, legendis, &c. Baleus de actis Rom. Pont.

275. Pleasing spectacles to the ignorant poor.

276. Th. Neageor.

277. Dum simulant spernere, acquisiverunt sibi 30 annorum spatio bis centena millia librarum annua. Arnold.

278. Et quum interdiu de virtute loquuti sunt, sero in latibulis clunes agitant labore nocturno, Agryppa.

279. 1 Tim. iii. 13. But they shall prevail no longer, their madness shall be known to all men.

280. Benignitatis sinus solebat esse, nunc litium officina curia Romana Budaeus.

281. Quid tibi videtur facturus Democritus, si horum spectator contigisset?

282. Ob inanes ditionum titulos, ob prereptum locum, ob interceptam mulierculam, vel quod e stultitia natum, vel e malitia, quod cupido dominandi, libido nocendi, &c.

283. Bellum rem plane bellui nam vocat Morus. Utop. lib. 2.

284. Munster. Cosmog. l. 5, c. 3. E. Dict. Cretens.

285. Jovius vit. ejus.

286. Comineus.

287. Lib. 3.

288. Hist. of the siege of Ostend, fol. 23.

289. Erasmus de bello. Ut placidum illud animal benevoletiae natum tam ferina vecordia in mutuam rueret perniciem.

290. Rich. Dinoth. praefat. Belli civilis Gal.

291. Jovius.

292. Dolus, asperitas, in justitia propria bellorum negotia. Tertul.

293. Trully.

294. Lucan.

295. Pater in filium, affinis in affinem, amicus in amicum, &c. Regio cum regione, regnum regno colliditur. Populus populo in mutuam perniciem, belluarum instar sanguinolente ruentium.

296. Libanii declam.

297. Ira enim et furor Bellonae consultores, &c. dementes sacerdotes sunt.

298. Bellum quasi bellua et ad omnia scelera furor immissus.

299. Gallorum decies centum millia ceciderunt. Ecclesiaris 20 millia fundamentis excisa.

300. Belli civilis Gal. l. 1. hoc ferali bello et caedibus omnia repleverunt,

et regnum amplissimum a fundamentis pene everterunt, plebis tot myriades gladio, bello, fame miserabiliter perierunt.

301. Pont. Huterus.

302. Comineus. Ut nullus non execretur et admiretur crudelitatem, et barbaram insaniam, quae inter homines eodem sub caelo natos, ejusdem linguae, sanguinis, religionis, exercebator.

303. Lucan.

304. Virg.

305. Bishop of Cuseo, an eyewitness.

306. Read Meteran of his stupend cruelties.

307. Hensius Austriaco.

308. Virg. Georg. impious war rages throughout the whole world

309. Jansenius Gallobelgicus 1596. Mundus furiosus, inscriptio libri.

310. Exercitat. 250. serm. 4.

311. Fleat Heraclitus an rideat Democritus.

312. Curae leves loquuntur, ingentes stupent.

313. Arma amens capio, nec sat rationis in armis.

314. Erasmus.

315. Pro Murena. Omnes urbanae res, omnia studia, omnis forensis laus et industria latet in tutela et praecidio bellicae virtutis, et simul atque increpuit suspicio tumultus, artes illico nostrae conticescunt.

316. Ser. 13.

317. Crudelissimos saevissimosque latrones, fortissimos haberi propugnatores, fidissimos duces habent, bruta persuasione donati.

318. Eobanus Hessus. Quibus omnis in armis vita placet, non ulla juvat nisi morte, nec ullam esse putant vitam, quae non assueverit armis.

319. Lib. 10. vit. Scanperbeg.

320. Nulli beatiores habiti, quam qui in praelus cecidissent. Brisonius de

rep. Persarum. l. 3. fol. 3. 44. Idem Lactantius de Romanis et Graecis. Idem Ammianus, lib. 23. de Parthis. Judicatur is solus beatus apud eos, qui in praelio fuderit animam. De Benef. lib. 2. c. 1.

321. Nat. quaest. lib. 3.

322. Boterus Amphitridion. Busbequius Turc. hist. Per caedes et sanguinem parare hominibus ascensum in coelum putant, Lactan. de falsa relig. l. 1. cap. 8.

323. Quoniam bella acerbissima dei flagella sunt quibus hominum pertinaciam punit, ea perpetua oblivione sepelienda potius quam memoriae mandanda plerique judicant. Rich. Dinoth. praef. hist. Gall.

324. Cruentam humani generis pestem, et perniciem divinitatis nota insigniunt.

325. Et quod dolendum, applausum habent et occursum viri tales.

326. Herculi eadem porta ad coelum patuit, qui magnam generis humani partem perdidit.

327. Virg. Aeneid. 7.

328. Hominicidium quum committunt singuli, crimen est, quum publice geritur, virtus vocatur. Cyprianus.

329. Seneca. Successful vice is called virtue.

330. Juven.

331. De vanit. scient. de princip. nobilitatis.

332. Juven. Sat. 4.

333. Pausa rapit, quod Natta reliquit. Tu pessimus omnium latro es, as Demetrius the Pirate told Alexander in Curtius.

334. Non ausi mutire, &c. Aesop.

335. Improbum et stultum, si divitem multos bonos viros in servitutem habentem, ob id duntaxat quod ei contingat aureorum numismatum cumulus, ut appendices, et additamenta numismatum. Morus Utopia.

336. Eorumque detestantur Utopienses insaniam, qui divinos honores iis impendunt, quos sordidos et avaros agnoscunt; non alio respectu honorantes, quam quod dites sint. Idem. lib. 2.

337. Cyp. 2 ad Donat. ep. Ut reus innocens pereat, sit nocens. Judex damnat foras, quod intus operatur.

338. Sidonius Apo.

339. Salvianus l. 3. de providen.

340. Ergo judicium nihil est nisi publica merces. Petronius. Quid faciant leges ubi sola pecunia regnat? Idem.

341. Hic arcentur haerediatatibus liberi, hic donatur bonis alienis, falsum consulit, alter testamentum corrumpit, &c. Idem.

342. Vexat censura columbas.

343. Plaut. mostel.

344. Idem.

345. Juven. Sat. 4.

346. Quod tot sint fures et mendici, magistratuum culpa fit, qui malos imitantur praeceptores, qui discipulos libentius verberant quam docunt. Morus, Utop. lib. 1.

347. Decernuntur furi gravia et horrenda supplicia, quum potius providendum multo foret ne fures sint, ne cuiquam tam dira furandi aut pereundi sit necessitas. Idem.

348. Boterus de augment. urb lib. 3. cap. 3.

349. E fraterno corde sanguinem eliciunt.

350. Milvus rapit ac deglubit.

351. Petronius de Crotone civit.

352. Quid forum? locus quo alius alium circumvenit.

353. Vastum chaos, larvarum emporium, theatrum hypocrisios, &c.

354. Nemo coelum, nemo jusjurandum, nemo Jovem pluris facit, sed omnes apertis oculis bona sua computant. Petron.

355. Plutarch, vit. ejus. Indecorum animatis ut calceis uti aut vitris, quae ubi fracta abjicimus, nam ut de meipso dicam, nec bovem senem vendideram, nedum hominem natu grandem laboris socium.

356. Jovius. Cum innumera illius beneficia rependere non posset aliter, interfici jussit.

357. Beneficia eo usque lata sunt dum videntur solvi posse, ubi multum, antevenere pro gratia odium redditur. Tac.

358. Paucis charior est fides quam pecunia. Salust.

359. Prima fere vota et cunctis, &c.

360. Et genus et formam regina pecunia donat. Quantum quisque sua nummorum servat in arca, tantum habet et fidei.

361. Non a peritia sed ab ornatu et vulgi vocibus habemur excellentes. Cardan. l. 2. de cons.

362. Perjurata suo postponit numina lucro, Mercator. Ut necessarium sit vel Deo displicere, vel ab hominibus contemni, vexari, negligi.

363. Qui Curios simulant et Bacchanalia vivunt.

364. Tragelapho similes vel centauris, sursum homines, deorsum equi.

365. Praeceptis suis coelum promittunt, ipsi interim pulveris terreni vilia mancipia.

366. Aeneas Silv.

367. Arridere homines ut saeviant, blandiri ut fallant. Cyp. ad Donatum.

368. Love and hate are like the two ends of a perspective glass, the one multiplies, the other makes less.

369. Ministri locupletiores iis quibus ministratur, servus majores opes habens quam patronus.

370. Qui terram colunt equi paleis pascuntur, qui otiantur caballi avena saginantur, discalceatus discurrit qui calces aliis facit.

371. Juven. Do you laugh? he is shaken by still greater laughter; he weeps also when he has beheld the tears of his friend.

372. Bodin, lib. 4. de repub. cap. 6.

373. Plinius l. 37. cap. 3. capillos habuit succineos, exinde factum ut omnes puellae Romanae colorem illum affectarent.

374. Odit damnatos. Juv.

375. Agrippa ep. 38. l. 7. Quorum cerebrum est in ventre, ingenium in patinis.

376. Psal. They eat up my people as bread.

377. Absumit haeres caecuba lignior servata centum clavibus, et mero distinguet pavimentis superbo, pontificum potiore coenis. Hor.

378. Qui Thaidem pingere, inflare tibiam, crispare crines.

379. Doctus spectare lacunar.

380. Tullius. Est enim proprium stultitiae aliorum cernere vitia, oblivisci suorum. Idem Aristippus Charidemo apud Lucianum Omnino stultitiae cujusdam esse puto, &c.

381. Execrari publice quod occulte agat. Salvianus lib. de pro. acres ulciscendis vitiis quibus ipsi vehementer indulgent.

382. Adamus eccl. hist. cap. 212. Siquis damnatus fuerit, laetus esse gloria est; nam lachrymas et planctum caeteraque compunctionum genera quae nos salubria censemus, ita abominantur Dani, ut nec pro peccatis nec pro defunctis amicis ulli fiere liceat.

383. Orbi dat leges foras, vix famulum regit sine strepitu domi.

384. Quicquid ego volo hoc vult mater mea, et quod mater vult, facit pater.

385. Oves, olim mite pecus, nunc tam indomitum et edax ut homines devorent, &c. Morus. Utop. lib. 1.

386. Diversos variis tribuit natura furores.

387. Democrit. ep. praed. Hos. dejerantes et potantes deprehendet, hos vomentes, illos litigantes, insidias molientes, suffragantes, venena miscentes, in amicorum accusationem subscribentes, hos gloria, illos ambitione, cupiditate, mente captos, &c.

388. Ad Donat. ep. 2. l. 1. O si posses in specula sublimi constitutus, &c.

389. Lib. 1. de nup. Philol. in qua quid singuli nationum populi quotidianis motibus agitarent, relucebat.

390. O Jupiter contingat mihi aurum haereditas, &c. Multos da Jupiter

annos, Dementia quanta est hominum, turpissima vota diis insusurrant, si quis admoverit aurem, conticescunt; et quod scire homines nolunt, Deo narrant. Senec. ep. 10. l. 1.

391. Plautus Menech. non potest haec res Hellebori jugere obtinerier.

392. Eoque gravior morbus quo ignotior periclitanti.

393. Quae laedunt oculos, festinas demere; si quid est animum, differs curandi tempus in annum. Hor.

394. Si caput, crus dolet, brachium, &c. Medicum accersimus, recte et honeste, si par etiam industria in animi morbis poneretur. Joh. Pelenus Jesuita. lib. 2. de hum. affec. morborumque cura.

395. Et quotusquisque tamen est qui contra tot pestes medicum requirat vel aegrotare se agnoscat? ebullit ira, &c. Et nos tamen aegros esse negamus. Incolumes medicum recusant. Praesens aetas stultitiam priscis exprobrat. Bud. de affec. lib. 5.

396. Senes pro stultis habent juvenes. Balth. Cast.

397. Clodius accusat maechos.

398. Omnium stultissimi qui auriculas studiose tegunt. Sat. Menip.

399. Hor. Epist. 2.

400. Prosper.

401. Statim sapiunt, statim sciunt, neminem reverentur, neminem imitantur, ipsi sibi exemplo. Plin. Epist. lib. 8.

402. Nulli alteri sapere concedit ne desipere videatur. Agrip.

403. Omnis orbis persechio a persis ad Lusitaniam.

404. 2 Florid.

405. August. Qualis in oculis hominum qui inversis pedibus ambulat, talis in oculis sapientum et angelorum qui sibi placet, aut cui passiones dominantur.

406. Plautus Menechmi.

407. Governor of Asnich by Caesar's appointment.

408. Nunc sanitatis patrocinium est insanientium turba. Sen.

409. Pro Roseio Amerino, et quod inter omnes constat insanissimus, nisi inter eos, qui ipsi quoque insaniunt.

410. Necesse est cum insanientibus furere, nisi solus relinqueris. Petronius.

411. Quoniam non est genus unum stultitiae qua me insanire putas.

412. Stultum me fateor, liceat concedere verum, Atque etiam insanum. Hor.

413. Odi nec possum cupiens nec esse quod odi. Ovid. Errore grato libenter omnes insanimus.

414. Amator scortum vitae praeponit, iracundus vindictam; fur praedam, parasitus gulam, ambitiosus honores, avarus opes, &c. odimus haec et accercimus. Cardan. l. 2. de conso.

415. Prov. xxvi. 11.

416. Although you call out, and confound the sea and sky, you still address a deaf man.

417. Plutarch. Gryllo. suilli homines sic Clem. Alex. vo.

418. Non persuadebis, etiamsi persuaseris.

419. Tully.

420. Malo cum illis insanire, quam cum aliis bene sentire.

421. Qui inter hos enutriuntur, non magis sapere possunt, quam qui in culina bene olere. Patron.

422. Persius.

423. Hor. 2. ser. which of these is the more mad.

424. Vesanum exagitant pueri, innuptaeque puellae.

425. Plautus.

426. Hor. l. 2. sat. 2. Superbam stultitiam Plinus vocat. 7. epist. 21. quod semel dixi, fixum ratumque sit.

427. 19 Multi sapientes proculdubio fuissent, si se non putassent ad sapientiae summum pervenisse.

428. Idem.

429. Plutarchus Solone. Detur sapientiori.

430. Tam praesentibus plena est numinibus, ut facilius possis Deum quam hominem invenire.

431. Pulchrum bis dicere non nocet.

432. Malefactors.

433. Who can find a faithful man? Prov. xx. 6.

434. In Psal. xlix. Qui momentanea sempiternis, qui delapidat heri absentis bona, mox in jus vocandus et damnandus.

435. Perquam ridiculum est homines ex animi sententia vivere, et quae Diis ingrata sunt exequi, et tamen a solis Diis vella solvos fieri, quum propriae salutis curam abjecerint. Theod. c. 6. de provid. lib. de curat. graec. affect.

436. Sapiens sibi qui imperiosus, &c. Hor. 2. ser. 7.

437. Conclus. lib. de vie. offer, certum est animi morbis laborantes pro mortuis consendos.

438. Lib. de sap. Ubi timor adest, sapientia adesse nequit.

439. He who is desirous is also fearful, and he who lives in fear never can be free.

440. Quid insanius Xerxe Hellespontum verberante, &c.

441. Eccl. xxi. 12. Where is bitterness, there is no understanding. Prov. xii. 16. An angry man is a fool.

442. B Tusc. Injuria in sapientem non cadit.

443. Hom. 6. in 2 Epist. ad Cor. Hominem te agnoscere nequeo, cum tanquam asinus recalcitres, lascivias ut taurus, hinnias ut equus post mulieres, ut ursus ventri indulgeas, quum rapias ut lupus, &c. at inquis formam hominis habeo, Id magis terret, quum feram humana specie videre me putem.

444. Epist. lib. 2. 13. Stultus semper incipit vivere, foeda hominum levitas, nova quotidie fundamenta vitae ponere, novas spes, &c.

445. De curial. miser. Stultus, qui quaerit quod nequit invenire, stultus qui quaerit quod nocet inventum, stultus qui cum plures habet calles, deteriorem deligit. Mihi videntur omnes deliri, amentes, &c.

446. Ep. Demagete.

447. Amicis nostris Rhodi dicito, ne nimium rideant, aut nimium tristes sint.

448. Per multum risum poteris cognoscere stultum. Offic. 3. c. 9.

449. Sapientes liberi, stulti servi, libertas est potestas, &c.

450. Hor. 2. ser. 7.

451. Juven. Good people are scarce.

452. Hypocrit.

453. Ut mulier aulica nullius pudens.

454. Epist. 33. Quando fatuo delectari volo, non est longe quaerendus, me video.

455. Primo contradicentium.

456. Lib. de causis corrupt. artium.

457. Actione ad subtil. in Scal. fol. 1226.

458. Lib. 1. de sap.

459. Vide miser homo, quia totum est vanitas, totum stultitia, totum dementia, quicquid facis in hoc mundo, praeter hoc solum quod propter Deum facis. Ser. de miser, hom.

460. In 2 Platonis dial. 1. de justo.

461. Dum iram et odium in Deo revera ponit.

462. Virg. 1. Eccl. 3.

463. Ps. inebriabuntur ab ubertate domus.

464. In Psal. civ. Austin.

465. In Platonis Tim. sacerdos Aegyptius.

466. Hor. vulgis insanum.

467. Patet ea diviso probabilis, &c. ex. Arist. Top. ib. l. c. 8. Rog. Bac. Epist. de secret. art. et nat. c. 8. non est judicium in vulgo.

468. De occult. Philosop. l. 1. c. 25 et 19. ejusd. l. Lib. 10. cap. 4.

469. See Lipsius epist.

470. De politai illustrium lib. 1. cap. 4. ut in humanis corporibus variae accidunt mutationes corporis, animique, sic in republica, &c.

471. Ubi reges philosophantur, Plato.

472. Lib. de re rust.

473. Vel publicam utilitatem: salus publica suprema lex esto. Beata civitas non ubi pauci beati, sed tota civitas beata. Plato quarto de republica.

474. Mantua vae miserae nimium vicina Cremonae.

475. Interdum a feris, ut olim Mauritania, &c.

476. Deliciis Hispaniae anno 1604. Nemo malus, nemo pauper, optimus quisque aetque ditissimus. Pie, sancteque vivebant summaque cum veneratione, et timore divino cultui, sacrisque rebus incumbebant.

477. Polit. l. 5. c. 3.

478. Boterus Polit. lib. 1. c. 1. Cum nempe princeps rerum gerendarum imperitus, segnis, oscitans, suique muneris immemor, aut fatuus est.

479. Non viget respublica cujus caput infirmatur. Salisburiensis, c. 22.

480. See Dr. Fletcher's relation, and Alexander Gaeninus' history.

481. Abundans omni divitiarum affluentia incolarum multitudine splendore ac potentia.

482. Not above 200 miles in length, 60 in breadth, according to Adricomius.

483. Romulus Amascus.

484. Sabellicus. Si quis incola vetus, non agnosceret, si quis peregrinus ingemisceret.

485. Polit. l. 5. c. 6. Crudelitas principum, impunitas scelerum, violatio legum, peculatus pecuniae publicae, etc.

486. Epist.

487. De increm. urb. cap. 20. subditi miseri, rebelles, desperati, &c.

488. R. Darlington. 1596. conclusio libri.

489. Boterus l. 9. c. 4. Polit. Quo fit ut aut rebus desperatis exulent, aut conjuratione subditorum crudelissime tandem trucidentur.

490. Mutuis odiis et caedibus exhausti, &c.

491. Lucra ex malis, scelerastisque causis.

492. Salust.

493. For most part we mistake the name of Politicians, accounting such as read Machiavel and Tacitus, great statesmen, that can dispute of political precepts, supplant and overthrow their adversaries, enrich themselves, get honours, dissemble; but what is this to the bene esse, or preservation of a Commonwealth?

494. Imperium suapte sponte corruit.

495. Apul. Prim. Flor. Ex innumerabilibus, pauci Senatores genere nobiles, e consularibus pauci boni, e bonis adhuc pauci eruditi.

496. Non solum vitia concipiunt ipsi principes, sed etiam infundunt in civitatem, plusque exemplo quam peccato nocent. Cic. l. de legibus.

497. Epist. ad Zen. Juven. Sat. 4. Paupertas seditionem gignit et maleficium, Arist. Pol. 2. c. 7.

498. Vicious domestic examples operate more quickly upon us when suggested to our minds by high authorities.

499. Salust. Semper in civitate quibus opes nullae sunt bonis invident, vetera odere, nova exoptant, odio suarum rerum mutari omnia petunt.

500. De legibus. profligatae in repub. disciplinae est indicium jurisperitorum numerus, et medicorum copia.

501. In praef. stud. juris. Multiplicantur nunc in terris ut locustae non patriae parentes, sed pestes, pessimi homines, majore ex parta superciliosi, contentiosi, &c. licitum latrocinium exercent.

502. Dousa epid. loquieleia turba, vultures togati.

503. Barc. Argen.

504. Juris consulti domus oraculum civitatis. Tully.

505. Lib. 3.

506. Lib. 3.

507. Lib. 1. de rep. Gallorum, incredibilem reipub. perniciem afferunt.

508. Polycrat. lib.

509. Is stipe contentus, et hi asses integros sibi multiplicari jubent.

510. Plus accipiunt tacere, quam nos loqui.

511. Totius injustitiae nulla capitalior, quam eorum qui cum maxime decipiunt, id agunt, ut boni viri esse videantur.

512. Nam quocunque modo causa procedat, hoc semper agitur, ut loculi impleantur, etsi avaritia nequit satiari.

513. Camden in Norfolk: qui si nihil sit litium e juris apicibus lites tamen serere callent.

514. Plutarch, vit. Cat. causas apud inferos quas in suam fidem receperunt, patrocinio suo tuebuntur.

515. Lib. 2. de Helvet. repub. non explicandis, sed moliendis controversiis operam dant, ita ut lites in multos annos extrabantur summa cum molestia utrisque; partis et dum interea patrimonia exhauriantur.

516. Lupum auribus tenent.

517. Hor.

518. Lib. de Helvet. repub. Judices quocunque pago constituunt qui amica aliqua transactione si fieri possit, lites tollant. Ego majorum nostrorum simplicitatem admiror, qui sic causas gravissimas composuerint, &c.

519. Clenard. l. 1. ep. Si quae controversiae utraque para judicem adit, is semel et simul rem transigit, audit: nec quid sit appellatio, lachrymosaeque morae noscunt.

520. Camden.

521. Lib. 10. epist. ad Atticum, epist. II.

522. Biblioth. l. 3.

523. Lib. de Anim.

524. Lib. major morb. corp. an animi. Hi non conveniunt ut diis more majorum sacra faciant, non ut Jovi primitias offerant, aut Baccho commessationes, sed anniversarius morbus exasperans Asiam huc eos coegit, ut contentiones hic peragant.

525. I Cor. vi. 5, 6.

526. Stulti quando demum sapietis? Ps. xlix. 8.

527. So intituled, and preached by our Regius Professor, D. Prideaux; printed at London by Felix Kingston, 1621.

528. Of which Text read two learned Sermons.

529. Saepius bona materia cessat sine artifice. Sabellicus de Germania. Si quis videret Germaniam urbibus hodie excultam, non diceret ut olim tristem cultu, asperam coelo, terram informem.

530. By his Majesty's Attorney General there.

531. As Zeipland, Bemster in Holland, &c.

532. From Gaunt to Sluce, from Bruges to the Sea, &c.

533. Ortelius, Boterus, Mercator, Meteranus, &c.

534. The citadel par excellance.

535. Jam inde non belli gloria quam humanitatis cultu inter florentissimas orbis Christiani gentes imprimis floruit. Camden Brit. de Normannis.

536. Georg. Kecker.

537. Tam hieme quam aestate intrepide sulcant Oceanum, et duo

illorum duces non minore audacia quam fortuna totius orbem terrae circumnavigarunt. Amphitheatro Boterus.

538. A fertile soil, good air, &c. Tin, Lead, Wool, Saffron, &c.

539. Tota Britannia unica velut arx Boter.

540. Lib. 1. hist.

541. Increment, urb. l. 1. c. 9.

542. Angliae, excepto Londino, nulla est civitas memorabilia, licet ea natio rerum omnium copia abundet.

543. Cosmog. Lib. 3. cop. 119. Villarum non est numerus, nullus locus otiosus aut incultus.

544. Chytreus orat. edit. Francof. 1583.

545. Maginus Geog.

546. Ortelius e Vaseo et Pet. de Medina.

547. An hundred families in each.

548. Populi multitudo diligente cultura foecundat solum. Boter. l. 8. c. 3.

549. Orat. 35. Terra ubi oves stabulantur optima agricolis ob stercus.

550. De re rust. l. 2. cap. 1. The soil is not tired or exhausted, but has become barren through our sloth.

551. Hodie urbibus desolatur, et magna ex parte incolis destituitur. Gerbelius desc. Graeciae, lib. 6.

552. Videbit eas fere omnes aut eversas, aut solo aequatas, aut in rudera foedissime dejectas Gerbelius.

553.

Not even the hardest of our foes could hear,

Nor stern Ulysses tell without a tear.

554. Lib. 7. Septuaginta olim legiones scriptae dicuntur; quas vires hodie, &c.

555. Polit. l. 3. c. 8.

556. For dyeing of cloths, and dressing, &c.

557. Valer. l. 2. c. 1.

558. Hist. Scot. Lib. 10. Magnis propositis praemiis, ut Scoti ab iis edocerentur.

559. Munst. cosm. l. 5. c. 74. Agro omnium rerum infoecundissimo aqua indigente inter saxeta, urbs tamen elegantissima, ob Orientis negotiationes et Occidentis.

560. Lib. 8. Georgr: ob asperum situm.

561. Lib. Edit. a Nic. Tregant. Belg. A. 1616. expedit. in Sinas.

562. Ubi nobiles probi loco habent artem aliquam profiteri. Cleonard. ep. l. 1.

563. Lib. 13. Belg. Hist. non tam laboriosi ut Belgae, sed ut Hispani otiatores vitam ut plurimum otiosam agentes: artes manuariae quae plurimum habent in se laboris et difficultatis, majoremque requirunt industriam, a peregrinis et exteris exercentur; habitant in piscosissimo mari, interea tantum non piscantur quantum insulae suffecerit sed a vicinis emere coguntur.

564. Grotii Liber.

565. Urbs animis numeroque potens, et robore gentis. Scaliger.

566. Camden.

567. York, Bristow, Norwich, Worcester, &c.

568. M. Gainsford's Argument: Because gentlemen dwell with us in the country villages, our cities are less, is nothing to the purpose: put three hundred or four hundred villages in a shire, and every village yield a gentleman, what is four hundred families to increase one of our cities, or to contend with theirs, which stand thicker? And whereas ours usually consist of seven thousand, theirs consist of forty thousand inhabitants.

569. Maxima pars victus in carne consistit. Polyd. Lib. 1. Hist.

570. Refraenate monopolii licentiam, pauciores alantur otio, redintegretur agricolatio, lanificium instauretur, ut sit honestum negotium quo se exerceat otiosa illa turba. Nisi his malis medentur, frustra exercent justitiam. Mor. Utop. Lib. 1.

571. Mancipiis locuples eget aeris Cappadocum rex. Hor.

572. Regis dignitatis non est exercere imperium in mendicos sed in opulentos. Non est regni decus, sed carceris esse custos. Idem.

573. Colluvies hominum mirabiles excocti solo, immundi vestes foedi visu, furti imprimis acres, &c.

574. Cosmog. lib. 3. cap. 5.

575. Let no one in our city be a beggar.

576. Seneca. Haud minus turpia principi multa supplicia, quam medico multa funera.

577. Ac pituitam et bilem a corpore (11. de leg.) omnes vult exterminari.

578. See Lipsius Admiranda.

579. De quo Suet. in Claudio, et Plinius, c. 36.

580. Ut egestati simul et ignaviae occurratur, opificia condiscantur, tenues subleventur. Bodin. l. 6. c. 2. num. 6,7.

581. Amasis Aegypti rex legem promulgavit, ut omnes subditi quotannis rationem redderent unde viverent.

582. Buscoldus discursu polit. cap. 2. whereby they are supported, and do not become vagrants by being less accustomed to labour.

583. Lib. 1. de increm. Urb. cap. 6.

584. Cap. 5. de increm. urb. Quas flumen, lacus, aut mare alluit.

585. Incredibilem commoditatem, vectura mercium tres fluvii navigabiles, &c. Boterus de Gallia.

586. Herodotus.

587. Ind. Orient. cap. 2. Rotam in medio flumine constituunt, cui ex pellibus animalium consutos uteres appendunt, hi dum rota movetur, aquam per canales, &c.

588. Centum pedes lata fossa 30. alta.

589. Contrary to that of Archimedes, who holds the superficies of all waters even.

590. Lib. 1. cap. 3.

591. Dion. Pausanias, et Nic. Gerbelius. Munster. Cosm. Lib. 4. cap. 36. Ut brevior foret navigatio et minus periculosa.

592. Charles the great went about to make a channel from the Rhine to the Danube. Bil. Pirkimerus descript. Ger. the ruins are yet seen about Wessenburg from Rednich to Altimul. Ut navigabilia inter se Occidentis et Septentrionis littora fierent.

593. Maginus Georgr. Simlerus de rep. Helvet. lib. 1. describit.

594. Camden in Lincolnshire, Fossedike.

595. Near St. Albans, which must not now be whispered in the ear.

596. Lilius Girald. Nat. comes.

597. Apuleius, lib. 4. Flor. Lar. familiaris inter homines aetatis suae cultus est, litium omnium et jurgiorum inter propinquos arbitrer et disceptator. Adversus iracundiam, invidiam, avaritiam, libidinem, ceteraque animi humani vitia et monstra philosophus iste Hercules fuit. Pestes eas mentibus exegit omnes, &c.

598. Votia navig.

599. Raggnalios, part 2, cap. 2, et part 3, c. 17.

600. Velent. Andreae Apolog. manip. 604.

601. Qui sordidus est, sordescat adhuc.

602. Hor.

603. Ferdinando Quir. 1612.

604. Vide Acosta et Laiet.

605. Vide patritium, lib. 8. tit. 10. de Instit. Reipub.

606. Sic Olim Hippodamus Milesius Aris. polit. cap. 11. et Vitruvius l. 1. c. ult.

607. With walls of earth, &c.

608. De his Plin. epist. 42. lib. 2. et Tacit. Annal. 13. lib.

609. Vide Brisonium de regno Perse lib. 3. de his et Vegetium, lib. 2. cap. 3. de Annona.

610. Not to make gold, but for matters of physic.

611. Bresonius Josephus, lib. 21. antiquit. Jud. cap. 6. Herod. lib. 3.

612. So Lod. Vives thinks best, Comineus, and others.

613. Plato 3. de leg. Aediles creari vult, qui fora, fontes, vias, portus, plateas, et id genus alia procurent. Vide Isaacum Pontanum de civ. Amstel. haec omnia, &c. Gotardum et alios.

614. De Increm. urb. cap. 13. Ingenue fateor me non intelligere cur ignobilius sit urbes bene munitas colere nunc quam olim, aut casae rusticae praesse quam urbi. Idem Urbertus Foliot, de Neapoli.

615. Ne tantillum quidem soli incultum relinquitur, ut verum sit ne pollicem quidem agri in his regionibus sterilem aut infoecundum reperiri. Marcus Hemingias Augustanus de regno Chinae, l. 1. c. 3.

616. M. Carew, in his survey of Cornwall, saith that before that country was enclosed, the husbandmen drank water, did eat little or no bread, fol. 66, lib. 1. their apparel was coarse, they went bare legged, their dwelling was correspondent; but since inclosure, they live decently, and have money to spend (fol. 23); when their fields were common, their wool was coarse, Cornish hair; but since inclosure, it is almost as good as Cotswol, and their soil much mended. Tusser. cap. 52 of his husbandry, is of his opinion, one acre enclosed, is worth three common. The country enclosed I praise; the other delighteth not me, for nothing of wealth it doth raise, &c.

617. Incredibilis navigiorum copia, nihilo pauciores in aquis, quam in continenti commorantur. M. Ricceus expedit. in Sinas, l. 1. c. 3.

618. To this purpose, Arist. polit. 2. c. 6. allows a third part of their revenues, Hippodamus half.

619. Ita lex Agraria olim Romae.

620. Hic segetes, illic veniunt felicius uvae, Arborei faetus alibi, atque injussa virescunt Graminia. Virg. 1. Georg.

621. Lucanus, l. 6.

622. Virg.

623. Joh. Valent. Andreas, Lord Verulam.

624. So is it in the kingdom of Naples and France.

625. See Contarenus and Osorius de rebus gestis Emanuelis.

626. Claudian l. 7. Liberty never is more gratifying than under a pious king.

627. Herodotus Erato lib. 6. Cum Aegyptiis Lacedemonii in hoc congruunt, quod eorum praecones, tibicines, coqui, et reliqui artifices, in paterno artificio succedunt, et coquus a coquo gignitur, et paterno opere perseverat. Idem Marcus polus de Quinzay. Idem Osorius de Emanuele rege Lusitano. Riccius de Sinia.

628. Hippol. a collibus de increm. urb. c. 20. Plato idem 7. de legibus, quae ad vitam necessaria, et quibus carere non possumus, nullum dependi vectigal, &c.

629. Plato 12. de legibus, 40. annos natos vult, ut si quid memorabile viderent apud exteros, hoc ipsum in rempub. recipiatur.

630. Simlerus in Helvetia.

631. Utopienses causidicos excludant, qui causas callide et vafre tractent et disputent. Iniquissimum censens hominem ullis obligari legibus, quae aut numerosioret sunt, quam ut perlegi queant, aut obscuriores quam ut a quovis possint intelligi. Volunt ut suam quisque causam agat, eamque referat Judici quam narraturus fuerat patrono, sic minus erit ambagum, et veritas facilius elicietur. Mor. Utop. l. 2.

632. Medici ex publico victum sumunt. Boter. l. 1. c. 5. de Aegyptiis.

633. De his lege Patrit. l. 3. tit. 8. de reip. Instit.

634. Nihil a clientibus patroni accipiant, priusquam lis finita est. Barel. Argen. lib. 3.

635. It is so in most free cities in Germany.

636. Mat. Riccius exped. in Sinas, l. 1. c. 5. de examinatione electionum copiose agit, &c.

637. Contar. de repub. Venet. l. 1.

638. Osor. l. 11. de reb. gest. Eman. Qui in literis maximos progressus fecerint maximis honoribus afficiuntur, secundus honoris gradus

militibus assignatur, postremi ordinis mechanicis, doctorum hominum judiciis in altiorem locum quisque praesertur, et qui a plurimis approbatur, ampliores in rep. dignitates consequitur. Qui in hoc examine primas habet, insigni per totam vitam dignitate insignitur, marchioni similis, aut duci apud nos.

639. Cedant arma togae.

640. As in Berne, Lucerne, Friburge in Switzerland, a vicious liver is uncapable of any office; if a Senator, instantly deposed. Simlerus.

641. Not above three years, Arist. polit. 5. c. 8.

642. Nam quis custodiet ipsos custodes?

643. Cytreus in Greisgeia. Qui non ex sublimi despiciant inferiores, nec ut bestias conculcent sibi subditos auctoritatis nomini, confisi, &c.

644. Sesellius de rep. Gallorum, lib. 1 & 2.

645. For who would cultivate virtue itself, if you were to take away the reward?

646. Si quis egregium aut bello aut pace perfecerit. Sesel. l. 1.

647. Ad regendam rempub. soli literati admittuntur, nec ad eam rem gratia magistratuum aut regis indigent, omnia explorata cujusque scientia et virtute pendent. Riccius lib. 1. cap. 5.

648. In defuncti locum eum jussit subrogari, qui inter majores virtute reliquis praeiret; non fuit apud mortales ullum excellentius certamen, aut cujus victoria magis esset expetenda, non enim inter celeres, celerrimo, non inter robustos robustissimo, &c.

649. Nullum videres vel in hac vel in vicinis regionibus pauperem, nullum obaeratum, &c.

650. Nullus mendicus apud Sinas, nemini sano quamvis oculis turbatus sit mendicare permittitur, omnes pro viribus laborare, coguntur, caeci molis trusatilibus versandis addicuntur, soli hospitiis gaudent, qui ad labores sunt inepti. Osor. l. 11. de reb. gest. Eman. Heming. de reg. Chin. l. 1. c. 3. Gotard. Arth. Orient. Ind. descr.

651. Alex. ab Alex. 3. c. 12.

652. Sic olim Romae Isaac. Pontan. de his optime. Aristot. l. 2. c. 9.

653. Idem Aristot. pol. 5. c. 8. Vitiosum quum soli pauperum liberi educantur ad labores, nobilium et divitum in voluptatibus et deliciis.

654. Quae haec injustitia ut nobilis quispiam, aut faenerator qui nihil agat, lautam et splendidam vitam agat, otio et deliciis, quum interim auriga, faber, agricola, quo respub. carere non potest, vitam adeo miseram ducat, ut pejor quam jumentorum sit ejus conditio? Iniqua resp. quae dat parasitis, adulatoribus, inanium voluptatum artificibus generosis et otiosis tanta munera prodigit, at contra agricolis, carbonariis, aurigis, fabris, &c. nihil prospicit, sed eorum abusa labore florentia aetatis fame penset et aerumnis, Mor. Utop. l. 2.

655. In Segovia nemo otiosus, nemo mendicus nisi per aetatem aut morbum opus facere non potest: nulli deest unde victum quaerat, aut quo se exerceat. Cypr. Echovius Delit. Hispan. Nullus Genevae otiosus, ne septennis puer. Paulus Heuzner Itiner.

656. Athenaeus, l. 12.

657. Simlerus de repub. Helvet.

658. Spartian. olim Romae sic.

659. He that provides not for his family, is worse than a thief. Paul.

660. Alfredi lex. utraque manus et lingua praecidatur, nisi eam capite redemerit.

661. Si quis nuptam stuprarit, virga virilis ei praeciditur; si mulier, nasus et auricula praecidatur. Alfredi lex. En leges ipsi Veneri Martique timendas.

662. 54 Pauperes non peccant, quum extrema necessitate coacti rem alienam capiunt. Maldonat. summula quaest. 8. art. 3. Ego cum illis sentio qui licere putant a divite clam accipere, qui tenetur pauperi subvenire. Emmanuel Sa. Aphor. confess.

663. 55 Lib. 2. de Reg. Persarum.

664. Lib. 24.

665. Aliter Aristoteles, a man at 25, a woman at 20. polit.

666. Lex olim Licurgi, hodie Chinensium; vide Plutarchum, Riccium, Hemmingium, Arniseum, Nevisanum, et alios de hac quaestione.

667. Alfredus.

668. Apud Lacones olim virgines fine dote nubebant. Boter. l. 3. c. 3.

669. 61 Lege cautum non ita pridem apud Venetos, ne quis Patritius dotem excederet 1500 coron.

670. 62 Bux. Synag. Jud. Sic. Judaei. Leo Afer Africae descript. ne sint aliter incontinentes ob reipub. bonum. Ut August. Caesar. orat. ad caelibes Romanos olim edocuit.

671. Morbo laborans, qui in prolem facile diffunditur, ne genus humanum foeda contagione laedatur, juventute castratur, mulieres tales procul a consortio virorum ablegantur, &c. Hector Boethius hist. lib. 1. de vet. Scotorum moribus.

672. Speciosissimi juvenes liberis dabunt operam. Plato 5. de legibus.

673. The Saxons exclude dumb, blind, leprous, and such like persons from all inheritance, as we do fools.

674. Ut olim Romani, Hispani hodie, &c.

675. Riccius lib. 11. cap. 5. de Sinarum. expedit. sic Hispani cogunt Mauros arma deponere. So it is in most Italian cities.

676. Idem Plato 12. de legibus, it hath ever been immoderate, vide Guil. Stuckium antiq. convival. lib. 1. cap. 26.

677. Plato 9. de legibus.

678. As those Lombards beyond Seas, though with some reformation, mons pietatis, or bank of charity, as Malines terms it, cap. 33. Lex mercat. part 2. that lend money upon easy pawns, or take money upon adventure for men's lives.

679. That proportion will make merchandise increase, land dearer, and better improved, as he hath judicially proved in his tract of usury, exhibited to the Parliament anno 1621.

680. Hoc fere Zanchius com. in 4 cap. ad Ephes. aequissimam vocat usuram, et charitati Christianae consentaneam, modo non exigant, &c. nec omnes dent ad foenus, sed ii qui in pecuniis bona habent, et ob aetatem, sexum, artis alicujus ignorantiam, non possunt uti. Nec omnibus, sed mercatoribus et iis qui honeste impendent, &c.

681. Idem apud Persas olim, lege Brisonium.

682. We hate the hawk, because he always lives in battle.

683. Idem Plato de legibus.

684. 30. Optimum quidem fuerat eam patribus nostris mentem a diis datam esse, ut vos Italiae, nos Africae imperio contenti essemus. Neque enim Sicilia aut Sardinia satis digna precio sunt pro tot classibus, &c.

685. Claudian.

686. Thucydides.

687. A depopulatione, agrorum incendiis, et ejusmodi factis immanibus. Plato.

688. Hungar. dec. 1. lib. 9.

689. Sesellius, lib. 2. de repub. Gal. valde enim est indecorum, ubi quod praeter opinionem accidit dicere, Non putaram, presertim si res praecaveri potuerit. Livius, lib. 1. Dion. lib. 2. Diodorus Siculus, lib. 2.

690. Peragit tranquilla potestas. Quod violenta nequit.—Claudian.

691. Bellum nec timendum nec provocandum. Plin. Panegyr. Trajano.

692. Lib. 3. poet. cap. 19.

693. Lib. 4. de repub. cap. 2.

694. Peucer. lib. 1. de divinat.

695. Camden in Cheshire.

696. Iliad. 6. lib.

697. Vide Puteani Comun, Goclenium de portentosis coenis nostrorum temporum.

698. Mirabile dictu est, quantum opsoniorum una domus singulis diebus absumat, sternuntur mensae in omnes pene horas calentibus semper eduliis. Descrip. Britan.

699. Lib. 1. de rep. Gallorum; quod tot lites et causae forenses, aliae ferantur ex aliis, in immensum producantur, et magnos sumptus requirant unde fit ut juris administri plerumque nobilium possessiones

adquirant, tum quod sumptuose vivant, et a mercatoribus absorbentur et splendissime vestiantur, &c.

700. Ter.

701. Amphit. Plant.

702. Paling. Filius ut fur.

703. Catus cum mure, duo galli simul in aede, Et glotes binae nunquam vivunt sine lite.

704. Res angusta domi.

705. When pride and beggary meet in a family, they roar and howl, and cause as many flashes of discontents, as fire and water, when they concur, make thunder-claps in the skies.

706. Plautus Aulular.

707. Lib. 7. cap. 6.

708. Pellitur in bellis sapientia, vigeritur res. Vetus proverbium, aut regem aut fatuum nasci oportere.

709. Lib. 1. hist. Rom. similes a. bacculorum calculis, secundum computantis arbitrium, modo aerei sunt, modo aurei; ad nutum regis nunc beati sunt nunc miseri.

710. Aerumnosique Solones in Sa. 3. De miser. curialium.

711. F. Dousae Epid. lib. 1. c. 13.

712. Hoc cognomento cohonestati Romae, qui caeteros mortales sapientia praestarent, testis Plin. lib. 7. cap. 34.

713. Insanire parant certa ratione modoque, mad by the book they, & c.

714. Juvenal. O Physicians! open the middle vein.

715. Solomon.

716. Communis irrisor stultitiae.

717. Wit whither wilt?

718. Scaliger exercitat. 324.

719. Vit. ejus.

720. Ennius.

721. Lucian. Ter mille drachmis olim empta; studens inde sapientiam adipiscetur.

722. Epist. 21. 1. lib. Non oportet orationem sapientis esse politam aut solicitam.

723. Lib. 3. cap. 13. multo anhelitu jactatione furentes pectus, frontem caedentes, &c.

724. Lipsius, voces sunt, praeterea nihil.

725. Lib. 30. plus mail facere videtur qui oratione quam qui praetio quemvis corrumpit: nam, &c.

726. In Gorg. Platonis.

727. In naugerio.

728. Si furor sit Lyaeus, &c. quoties furit, furit, furit, amans, bibens, et Poeta, &c.

729. They are borne in the bark of folly, and dwell in the grove of madness.

730. Morus Utop. lib. 11.

731. Macrob. Satur. 7. 16.

732. Epist. 16.

733. Lib. de causis corrup. artium.

734. Lib. 2. in Ausonium, cap. 19 et 32.

735. Edit. 7. volum. Jano Gutero.

736. Aristophanis Ranis.

737. Lib. de beneficiis.

738. Delirus et amens dicatur merit. Hor. Seneca.

739. Ovid. Met. Majesty and Love do not agree well, nor dwell together.

740. Plutarch. Amatorio est amor insanus.

741. Epist. 39.

742. Sylvae nuptialis, l. 1. num. 11. Omnes mulieres ut plurimum stultae.

743. Aristotle.

744. Dolere se dixit quod tum vita egrederetur.

745. Lib. 1. num. 11. sapientia et divitiae vix simul possideri possunt.

746. They get their wisdom by eating piecrust some.

747. χρήματα τοῖς θνητοῖς γίνετω αφροσυνη. Opes quidem mortalibus sunt amentia. Theognis.

748. Fortuna nimium quem fovet, stultum facit.

749. Joh. 28.

750. Mag. moral. lib. 2 et lib. 1. sat. 4.

751. Hor. lib. 1. sat. 4.

752. Insana gula, insanae obstructiones, insanum venandi studium discordia demens. Virg. Aen.

753. Heliodorus Carthaginensis ad extremum orbis sarcophago testamento me hic jussi condier, et ut viderem an quis insanior ad me visendum usque ad haec loca penetraret. Ortelius in Gad.

754. If it be his work, which Gasper Veretus suspects.

755. Livy, Ingentes virtutes ingentia vitia.

756. Hor. Quisquis ambitione mala aut argenti pallet amore, Quisquis luxuria, tristique superstitione. Per.

757. Cronica Slavonica ad annum 1257. de cujus pecunia jam incredibilia dixerunt.

758. A fool and his money are soon parted.

759. Orat. de imag. ambitiosus et audax naviget Anticyras.

760. Navis stulta, quae continuo movetur nautae stulti qui se periculis

exponunt, aqua insana quae sic fremit, &c. aer jactatur, &c. qui mari se committit stolidum unum terra fugiens, 40. mari invenit. Gaspar Ens. Moros.

761. Cap. de alien. mentis.

762. Dipnosophist. lib. 8.

763. Tibicines mente Capti. Erasm. Chi. 14. cer. 7.

764. Prov. 30. Insana libido, Hic rogo non furor est, non est haec mentula demens. Mart. ep. 74. 1. 3.

765. Mille puellarum et puerorum mille jurores.

766. Uter est insanior horum. Hor. Ovid. Virg. Plin.

767. Plin. lib. 36.

768. Tacitus 3. Annal.

769. Ovid. 7. met. E. fungis nati homines ut olim Corinthi primaevi illius loci accolae, quia stolidi et fatui fungis nati dicebantur, idem et alibi dicas.

770. Famian. Strade de bajulis, de marmore semisculpti.

771. Arianus periplo maris Euxini portus ejus meminit, et Gillius, 1. 3. de Bospher. Thracio et laurus insana quae allata in convivium convivas omnes insania affecit. Guliel. Stucchius comment, &c.

772. Lepidum poema sic inscriptum.

773. No one is wise at all hours,—no one born without faults,—no one free from crime,—no one content with his lot,—no one in love wise,—no good, or wise man perfectly happy.

774. Stultitiam simulare non potes nisi taciturnitate.

775. Extortus non cruciatur, ambustus non laeditur, prostratus in lucta, non vincitur; non fit captivus ab hoste venundatus. Et si rugosus, senex edentulus, luscus, deformis, formosus tamen, et deo similis, felix, dives, rex nullius egens, et si denario non sit dignus.

776. Illum contendunt non injuria affici, non insania, non inebriari, quia virtus non eripitur ob constantes comprehensiones. Lips. phys. Stoic, lib. 3. diffi. 18.

777. Tarreus Hebus epig. 102. l. 8.

778. Hor.

779. Fratres sanct. Roseae crucis.

780. An sint, quales sint, unde nomen illud asciverint.

781. Turri Babel.

782. Omnium artium et scientiarum instaurator.

783. Divinus ille vir auctor notarum. in epist. Rog. Bacon. ed. Hambur. 1608.

784. Sapientiae desponsati.

785. From the Rising Sun to the Maeotid Lake, there was not one that could fairly be put in comparison with them.

786. Solus hic est sapiens alii volitant velut umbrae.

787. In ep. ad Balthas. Moretum.

788. Rejectiunculae ad Patavum. Felinus cum reliquis.

789. Magnum virum sequi est sapere, some think; others desipere. Catul.

790. Plant. Menec.

791. In Sat. 14.

792. Or to send for a cook to the Anticyrae to make Hellebore pottage, settle-brain pottage.

793. Aliquantulum tamen inde me solabor, quod una cum multis et sapientibus et celeberrimis viris ipse insipiens sim, quod se Menippus Luciani in Necyomantia.

794. Petronius in Catalect.

795. That I mean of Andr. Vale. Apolog. Manip. l. 1 et 26. Apol.

796. Haec affectio nostris temporibus frequentissima.

797. Cap. 15. de Mel.

798. De anima. Nostro hoc saeculo morbus frequentissimus.

799. Consult. 98. adeo nostris temporibus frequenter ingruit ut nullus fere ab ejus labe immunis reperiatur et omnium fere morborum occasio existat.

800. Mor. Encom si quis calumnietur levius esse quam decet Theologum, aut mordacius quam deceat Christianum.

801. Hor. Sat. 4. l. 1.

802. Epi. ad Dorpium de Moria. si quispiam offendatur et sibi vindicet, non habet quod expostulet cum eo scripsit, ipse si volet, secum agat injuriam, utpote sui proditor, qui declaravit hoc ad se proprie pertinere.

803. Si quis se laesum clamabit, aut conscientiam prodit suam, aut certe metum, Phaedr. lib. 3. Aesop. Fab.

804. If any one shall err through his own suspicion, and shall apply to himself what is common to all, he will foolishly betray a consciousness of guilt.

805. Hor.

806. Mart. l. 7. 22.

807. Ut lubet feriat, abstergant hos ictus Democriti pharmacos.

808. Rusticorum dea preesse vacantibus et otiosis putabatur, cui post labores agricola sacrificabat. Plin. l. 3. c. 12. Ovid. l. 6. Fast. Jam quoque cum fiunt antiquae sacra Vacunae, ante Vacunales stantque sedentque focos. Rosinus.

809. Ter. prol. Eunuch.

810. Ariost. l. 39. Staf. 58.

811. Ut enim ex studiis gaudium sic studia ex hilaritate proveniunt. Plinius Maximo suo, ep. lib. 8.

812. Annal. 15.

813. Sir Francis Bacon in his Essays, now Viscount St. Albans.

814. Quod Probus Persii βιογραφος virginali verecundia Persium fuisse dicit, ego, &c.

815. Quas aut incuria fudit, aut humana parum cavit natura. Hor.

816. Prol. quer. Plaut. Let not any one take these things to himself, they are all but fictions.

817. Si me commorit, melius non tangere clamo. Hor.

818. Hippoc. epist. Damageto, accercitus sum ut Democritum tanquam insanum curarem, sed postquam conveni, non per Jovem desipientiae negotium, sed rerum omnium receptaculum deprehendi, ejusque ingenium demiratus sum. Abderitanos vero tanquam non sanos accusavi, veratri potione ipsos potius eguisse dicens.

819. Mart.

Printed in Great Britain
by Amazon